AF365447

Tailored Travel GUIDES

UNVEILING
ROME

Your Travel Guide to The Eternal City

ESSENTIALS EDITION

ITALY UNCOVERED SEARIES

Presented by

Discover Your Journey

WEST AGORA INT
Timișoara 2024
www.tailoredtravelguides.com
WEST AGORA INT S.R.L. All Rights Reserved

Descrierea CIP a Bibliotecii Nationale a Romaniei
TAILORED TRAVEL GUIDES
Unveiling Rome - ITALY: Your Travel Guide to The Eternal
City / Tailored Travel Guides - Essentials edition - Timisoara:
West Agora Int, 2024
ISBN 978-606-95923-0-4
913

W I K I

Rome: The Eternal City of History, Art, and Civilization

Rome, the capital of Italy, stands as a timeless testament to the grandeur of human civilization. Known as the "Eternal City," Rome's history spans over 28 centuries, making it one of the oldest continuously occupied sites in Europe. Founded in 753 BC, according to tradition, by Romulus and Remus, Rome grew from a small Latin village to the heart of the mighty Roman Empire, exerting immense influence over the world in terms of politics, culture, and religion.

The city's historical significance is unparalleled, marked by its central role in the Roman Republic, the Roman Empire, and later as the seat of the Papacy. Rome's ancient heritage is showcased in iconic landmarks like the Colosseum, the Roman Forum, and the Pantheon, each a marvel of architectural and engineering prowess. The fall of the Roman Empire led to a period of decline, but Rome reemerged as a powerful city during the Renaissance and the Baroque periods, leaving a legacy of artistic and architectural masterpieces.

Rome is not just a relic of the past; it is a living museum where history is woven into the fabric of modern life. The Vatican City, an independent city-state enclaved within Rome, is the spiritual and administrative center of the Roman Catholic Church and home to the Pope. It boasts some of the world's most sacred sites and art treasures, including St. Peter's Basilica and the Sistine Chapel, adorned with Michelangelo's breathtaking frescoes.

The city's culinary scene reflects its rich cultural heritage, offering a fusion of traditional Italian cuisine with local Roman flavors. Dishes like carbonara and amatriciana are not just meals but a part of Rome's identity.

The city's vibrant neighborhoods, from the historic Trastevere to the trendy Monti, offer a glimpse into the daily life of Romans, blending the ancient with the contemporary.

Rome's commitment to preserving its vast historical and cultural heritage is evident in its meticulous care of ancient sites and its efforts to balance the preservation of its past with the needs of a modern European capital. The city faces challenges in managing tourism, urban development, and protecting its archaeological treasures.

Rome has been home to some of history's most influential figures, including Julius Caesar, Augustus, and countless artists and thinkers of the Renaissance. It has also been the center of significant events and movements, from the rise and fall of the Roman Empire to the unification of Italy.

Today, Rome stands as a symbol of the enduring legacy of human achievement. It is a city that offers an unparalleled journey through time, where every street, building, and ruin tells a story of a civilization that has shaped the world. For those seeking to immerse themselves in the depths of history, art, and culture, Rome offers an experience that transcends time, captivating the imagination and inspiring awe at every turn.

CONTENTS

ROME

THE ETERNAL CITY

Rome, Italy: a city where history and modernity intertwine in a vibrant tapestry, Rome stands as a testament to the grandeur of ancient civilizations and the enduring allure of Italian culture. Known as the "Eternal City," Rome's streets echo with the tales of emperors, artists, and philosophers who shaped the Western world. This is a city where awe-inspiring monuments, such as the Colosseum and the Pantheon, coexist with bustling piazzas and charming trattorias. Rome's rich historical legacy is matched only by its dynamic present, making it a destination that captivates the hearts of travelers from around the world.

In this guide, you will embark on a journey through Rome's captivating landscapes, from its iconic landmarks and hidden gems to its lush gardens and culinary delights. Each section is crafted to offer you a comprehensive understanding of what makes Rome unique, providing practical tips, cultural insights, and local recommendations. Whether you're marveling at the Sistine Chapel's masterpieces, exploring the cobbled lanes of Trastevere, or indulging in authentic Roman cuisine, this guide aims to make your Roman holiday an unforgettable experience.

As you navigate through the chapters, imagine the stories these ancient streets could tell and the secrets they keep. Rome is not just a destination; it's an experience that will stay with you long after you've returned home. So, let's embark on this adventure together, exploring the heart and soul of Rome, Italy.

GREETINGS AND INSIGHTS FROM LOCALS

Benvenuto, dear traveler! Welcome to Rome, the Eternal City, where history unfolds at every corner and modern vibrancy pulses through ancient streets. As a true Romano, I've walked beneath the shadows of the Colosseum and basked in the splendor of the Vatican, and I am thrilled to share with you the intimate corners and timeless experiences that only a local would cherish.

Embark on your Roman odyssey by embracing our storied traditions. A heartfelt "buongiorno" and a warm smile are your keys to unlocking the eternal treasures of this city as you wander through layers of history, from the majestic ruins of the Forum to the baroque elegance of Piazza Navona.

You might find yourself entranced by the allure of the Vatican Museums. Here, art and history converge in a breathtaking display of human creativity, from the intricate tapestries to the divine beauty of the Sistine Chapel, each corner a testament to the city's artistic legacy.

For a taste of authentic Roman life, meander through the bustling Trastevere neighborhood. Amid its cobbled alleys and ivy-draped facades, indulge in the culinary delights of the city – from savory supplì to a classic carbonara, each bite a symphony of flavors.

When the call of history beckons, make your way to the Pantheon. Its ancient dome, a marvel of architectural ingenuity, has watched over Rome for centuries, offering a haven of tranquility amidst the city's lively pace.

As twilight drapes its golden hues, the Spanish Steps beckon. This iconic spot, with its Baroque elegance and the gentle murmur of the Trevi Fountain nearby, becomes a magical stage for both lovers and dreamers alike under the starlit sky.

In the heart of Rome, the Colosseum stands as a monumental testament to the city's imperial past. Its towering arches and vast arena evoke images of ancient gladiators, a symbol of Rome's enduring legacy.

Rome's true essence lies in its harmonious blend of the past and the present, where every corner tells a story. We, the Romans, are here with open arms, eager to share the secrets and wonders of our beloved city with you. Arrivederci, dear traveler, and may your journey through Rome be an unforgettable voyage through time!

PRACTICAL INFORMATION

Currency

In Rome, as in all of Italy, the official currency is the Euro (€). Cash is commonly used, especially in smaller establishments and markets, but credit and debit cards are widely accepted. ATMs, known locally as Bancomats, are readily available throughout the city.

Transportation

Rome's public transportation system includes buses, trams, metro, and urban railways. The Metropolitana (metro) has three lines (A, B, and C) and is the quickest way to travel long distances. Tickets are valid across the network and can be purchased at stations, tobacco shops, and some bars. Taxis are reliable but can be expensive; they can be hailed on the street or found at designated taxi stands.

Driving in Rome

Driving in Rome can be challenging due to heavy traffic, limited parking, and ZTL zones (restricted traffic areas). It's recommended to use public transport or taxis when moving around the city. If you do need to drive, be sure to check ZTL restrictions and parking options.

Climate

Rome enjoys a Mediterranean climate. Summers (June-August) are hot and dry, while winters (December-February) are mild and wet. The best times to visit are spring (April-June) and autumn (September-October), when the weather is pleasant and the crowds are smaller.

PRACTICAL INFORMATION

Language

Italian is the official language. English is widely spoken in tourist areas, but learning a few basic Italian phrases can enhance your experience.

Power sockets and adapters

Italy uses type C, F, and L power sockets, and the standard voltage is 230V. Travelers from most countries will need a power adapter.

Shopping

Rome offers a variety of shopping experiences, from luxury designer boutiques on Via Condotti to artisanal shops in Trastevere. Shops typically open around 10 am and close at 8 pm, with a break in the afternoon.

Tipping

Tipping in Rome is not obligatory but appreciated for good service. In restaurants, a service charge may be included in the bill; otherwise, a tip of 5-10% is customary. For taxi drivers, rounding up to the nearest euro is common.

PRACTICAL INFORMATION

USEFUL LINKS AND PHONE NUMBERS

Emergency Services

All Emergencies: 112
Police (Carabinieri): 112
Local Police (Polizia): 113
Fire Brigade (Vigili del Fuoco): 115
Medical Emergencies (Pronto Soccorso): 118

Transportation

Rome's Main Airport (Fiumicino - Leonardo da Vinci International Airport): +39 06 65951, www.adr.it/web/aeroporti-di-roma-en/
Rome's Secondary Airport (Ciampino - G.B. Pastine International Airport): +39 06 65951, www.adr.it/web/aeroporti-di-roma-en/pax-cia-ciampino
ATAC (Public Transport in Rome): +39 06 57003, www.atac.roma.it/en/home
Trenitalia (National Railway Company): +39 06 68475475, www.trenitalia.com/en.html
Taxi Service: +39 06 0609, www.comune.roma.it/web/it/welcome.page

Tourist Information

Rome Tourist Board: +39 060608 (every day 9.00 am - 7.00 pm), www.turismoroma.it/en
Vatican Tourist Information: +39 06 69884676, www.vatican.va/content/vatican/en.html

Hospitals

Policlinico Umberto I: +39 06 49971, www.policlinicoumberto1.it
Ospedale Pediatrico Bambino Gesù (Children's Hospital): +39 06 68591, www.ospedalebambinogesu.it

Local Government

Rome City Council: +39 06 0606, www.comune.roma.it
Cultural Heritage Department: +39 06 0608, www.sovraintendenzaroma.it

Maps

For print versions - quick acces through QR codes after the End Note

Rome maps: www.ontheworldmap.com/italy/city/rome/
Rome General Map: www.ontheworldmap.com/italy/city/rome/large-detailed-street-map-of-rome.jpg
Rome Tourist Map: www.ontheworldmap.com/italy/city/rome/detailed-tourist-map-of-rome.jpg
Rome City Center Map: www.ontheworldmap.com/italy/city/rome/rome-city-centre-map.jpg
Rome Sightseeing Map: www.ontheworldmap.com/italy/city/rome/rome-sightseeing-map.jpg
Rome and surroundings Transport Map: www.ontheworldmap.com/italy/city/rome/transport-map-of-rome-and-the-surrounding-area.jpg
Rome Railway Map: www.ontheworldmap.com/italy/city/rome/rome-railway-map.jpg

PRACTICAL INFORMATION
ROME AND SURROUNDINGS

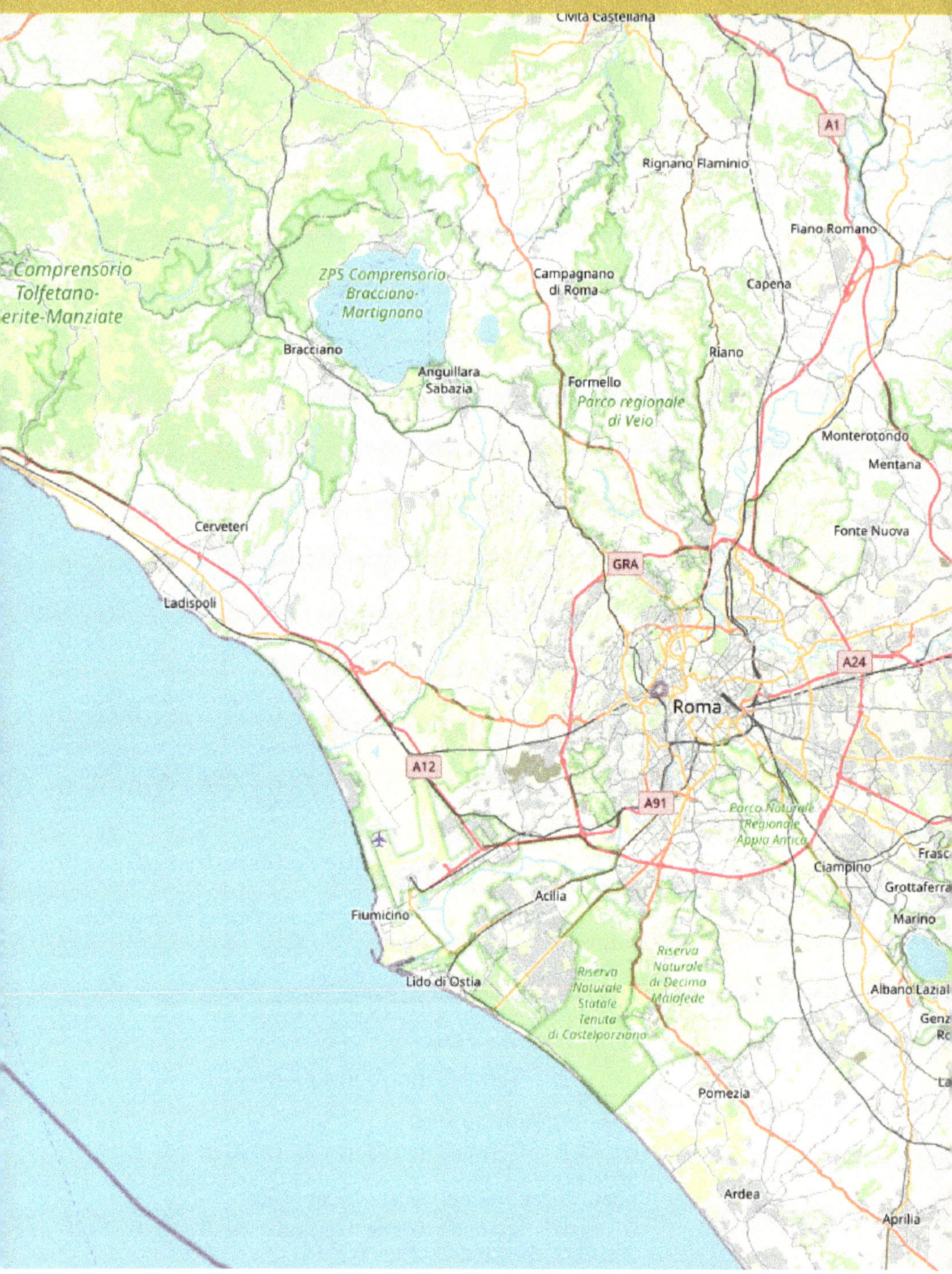

PRACTICAL INFORMATION
ROME AND SURROUNDINGS

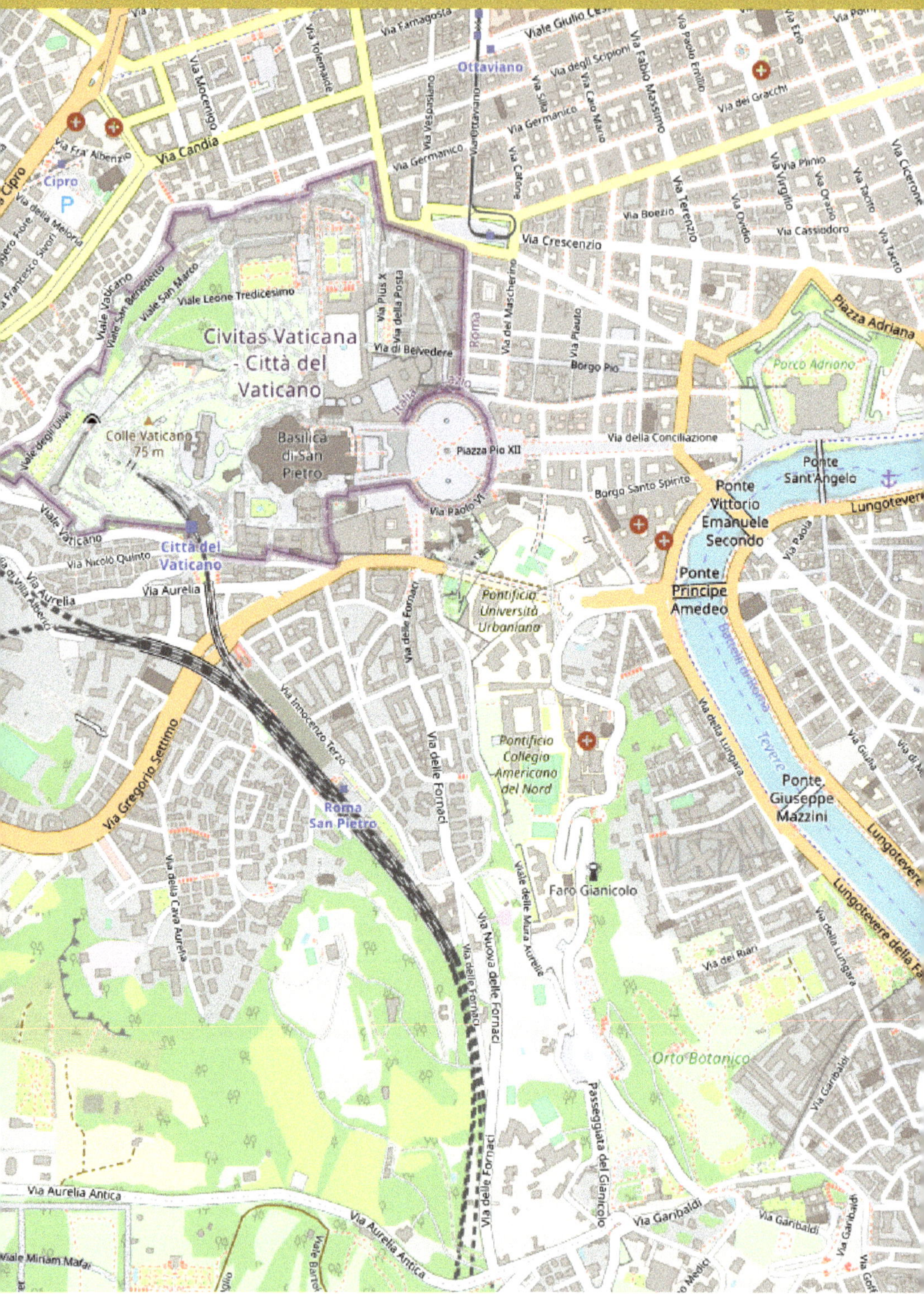
Via Famagosta
Viale Giulio Cesare
Ottaviano
Via degli Scipioni
Via Fabio Massimo
Via Paolo Emilio
Via Ezio
Via dei Gracchi
Via Fra' Albenzio
Via Candia
Via Mocenigo
Via Tolemaide
Via Vespasiano
Via Ottaviano
Via Silla
Via Germanico
Via Cola di Rienzo
Via Caio Mario
Via Germanico
Via Catone
Via Boezio
Via Terenzio
Via Plauto
Via Crescenzio
Via Cicerone
Via Virgilio
Via Pinio
Via Orazio
Via Tacito
Via Ovidio
Via Cassiodoro
Via Tacio
Cipro
Cipro
Via Francesco Sivori
Fiore della Meloria
Viale Vaticano
Viale San Gregorio
Viale San Benedetto
Viale San Marco
Viale Leone Tredicesimo
Via Pius X
Via della Posta
Via di Belvedere
Roma
Via del Mascherino
Borgo Pio
Piazza Adriana
Porto Adriano
Civitas Vaticana
Città del
Vaticano
Italia
Lazio
Via della Conciliazione
Ponte
Sant'Angelo
Lungotevere
Colle Vaticano
75 m
Viale degli Olivi
Basilica
di San
Pietro
Piazza Pio XII
Borgo Santo Spirito
Ponte
Vittorio
Emanuele
Secondo
Via Paola
Viale Vaticano
Via Paolo VI
Città del
Vaticano
Via Nicolò Quinto
Via Aurelia
Ponte
Principe
Amedeo
Via Aurelia
Pontificia
Università
Urbaniano
Via di Villa Abberici
Via delle Fornaci
Banchi Nuovi
Via della Lungara
Via Giulia
Via di
Tevere
Via Innocenzo Terzo
Pontificio
Collegio
Americano
del Nord
Ponte
Giuseppe
Mazzini
Via Gregorio Settimo
Via delle Fornaci
Via della Cava Aurelia
Roma
San Pietro
Via delle Mura Aurelia
Lungotevere
Faro Gianicolo
Via dei Riari
Lungotevere della Fa
Via della Lungara
Via Nuova delle Fornaci
Passeggiata del Gianicolo
Orto Botanico
Via Garibaldi
Via Aurelia Antica
Viale Miriam Mafai
Viale Bartol
Via Aurelia Antica
Via delle Fornaci
Via Garibaldi
Via Garibaldi
Via Goff

Villa Borghese
Giardino di Villa Medici
Via del Babuino
Via del Corso
Via del Greco
Via Margutta
Via Vittoria
Via di Ripetta
Passeggiata di Ripetta
Lungotevere dei Mellini
Lungotevere Marzio
Lungotevere in Braga
Ponte Cavour
Via di Monte Brianzo
Via dell'Orso
Via della Scrofa
Via di Ripetta
Via Bethania
Via Mario de' Fiori
Piazza di Spagna
Via del Condotti
Via Frattina
Via della Vite
Via della Mercede
Via del Corso
Spagna
Via di Porta Pinciana
Via Lombardia
Via Ludovisi
Via Ludovisi
Via Sistina
Via Gregoriana
Via Zucchelli
Via del Tritone
Via Marche
Via Emilia
Via Sardegna
Via Toscana
Via Sicilia
Via Abruzzi
Via Boncompagni
Via Piemonte
Via Molise
Via di San Basilio
Via Sallustiana
Via Giosue Cardu
Via di San Nicola da Tolentino
Via Barberini
Barberini
Via del Tritone
Via Rasella
Via dei Giardini
Via Firenze
Via Modena
Via Nazion
Trafora Umberto Primo
Via del Quirinale
Via Piacenza
Via Milano
Via Parma
Via Palermo
Via del Boschetto
Via Mazzarino
Via Cimarra
Via Panisperna
Via dei Capocci
Via Urbana
Via dei Serpenti
Via Baccina
Via Cesare B
Cavour
Via del Fagutale
Via dei Pastini
Piazza Navona
Via Monterone
Via del Corso
Via dei Giubbonari
Via Arenula
Telle Zoccolette
evere dei Vallati
Lungotevere De' Cenci
Ponte Garibaldi
Tevere
Isola Tiberina
Via della Luce
Ponte Palatino
Roma
Via di San Teodoro
Via Sacra
Via Sacra
Via Nova
Via Sacra
Colosseo
Piazza del Colosseo
Piazza del Colosseo
Via Celio Vibenna
Viale

TOP ATTRACTIONS IN ROME

COLOSSEUM

The Colosseum, a monumental testament to Roman engineering and architectural mastery, stands as a symbol of the Eternal City's ancient grandeur. Known initially as the Flavian Amphitheatre, it was erected in 70-80 AD and remains the largest amphitheater in the world. The Colosseum could accommodate up to 80,000 spectators, who gathered to witness spectacles of gladiatorial combat, exotic animal hunts, and mock naval battles. The structure's complex design included the hypogeum, an elaborate underground network of passages and rooms where gladiators and animals were held before contests. This architectural wonder, despite centuries of wear and partial destruction, continues to awe visitors with its enduring beauty and historical significance.

Tip: To enhance your experience, consider booking a guided tour that includes access to the Colosseum's underground chambers, arena floor, and upper tiers. These areas provide unique perspectives and insights into the amphitheater's history and function. Early morning or late afternoon visits are recommended to avoid the peak tourist crowds and to experience the Colosseum in different lights. Additionally, check for night tours for a unique and less crowded experience.

Location: Piazza del Colosseo, 1, 00184 Roma RM

Website: https://colosseo.it/

VATICAN CITY

Vatican City, the heart of Roman Catholicism and the smallest independent state in the world, is an enclave of immense religious and cultural significance within Rome. As the papal residence, it houses stunning masterpieces of art and architecture. The Vatican Museums offer an unparalleled collection, including ancient Roman sculptures, priceless Renaissance art, and, notably, the Sistine Chapel adorned with Michelangelo's breathtaking frescoes. St. Peter's Basilica, another jewel in the Vatican's crown, captivates visitors with its magnificent dome designed by Michelangelo, its opulent interior, and the revered Pietà statue. The beauty and sanctity of Vatican City make it a must-visit destination, offering a deeply moving experience that transcends religious boundaries.

Tip: To fully appreciate the vastness and richness of Vatican City, allocate a good portion of your day for the visit. Guided tours, including those of the Vatican Gardens and the necropolis beneath St. Peter's Basilica, can greatly enrich your experience. Remember, the dress code is strict for religious sites; appropriate attire covering shoulders and knees is required. Also, consider visiting the Vatican early in the morning or late in the afternoon to avoid the crowds, and pre-book your tickets online to skip the long entry lines.

Location: 00120 Vatican City

Website: www.museivaticani.va

PANTHEON

The Pantheon stands as a monumental symbol of ancient Roman architectural brilliance and enduring grandeur. Originally built as a temple to all gods around 126 AD, it was later converted into a Christian church. The Pantheon is renowned for its architectural features, notably its massive dome, the largest unreinforced concrete dome in the world, crowned with a central oculus that bathes the interior in natural light. This engineering marvel has stood the test of time, largely intact, offering a glimpse into the Roman Empire's advanced architectural capabilities. The interior, marked by elegant Corinthian columns and a coffered dome, is also notable as the final resting place of illustrious Italians, including the Renaissance artist Raphael and several Italian kings. The Pantheon's harmony of proportions and the awe-inspiring dome provide an unforgettable experience, encapsulating the essence of Roman architectural and cultural influence.

Tip: While entry to the Pantheon is free, it's advisable to visit early in the morning or late in the afternoon to avoid the crowds. The Pantheon is an active church with occasional religious services and events, so visitors should dress respectfully and maintain a quiet demeanor inside. The oculus, especially during a rain shower or on a bright day, offers a spectacular view, creating a unique play of light and shadows within the ancient walls.

Location: Piazza della Rotonda, 00186 Roma RM, Italy

Website: www.pantheonroma.com

ROMAN FORUM

The Roman Forum, the nucleus of ancient Roman civilization, is an expansive area brimming with ruins that once formed the center of Roman public and political life. This archaeological marvel was the site of monumental events, from triumphal processions and pivotal elections to public speeches that swayed the course of history. Walking through the Forum, visitors are transported back in time as they wander among the remnants of significant structures like the Senate House, the Temple of Saturn, and the Arch of Titus. Each ruin tells a story of a civilization that has profoundly influenced the modern world. The Roman Forum offers not just a walk through ancient ruins but an immersive journey into the lives of the Romans who shaped history in this very place.

Tip: To truly appreciate the historical significance of the Forum, consider hiring a guide or using an audio guide (available at website) for detailed insights into each structure's history and importance. The area can be quite vast and overwhelming, so wearing comfortable walking shoes is recommended. Visiting early in the morning or late in the afternoon not only helps in avoiding the crowds but also offers softer light for photography, casting dramatic shadows across the ancient stones. A combined ticket with the Colosseum and Palatine Hill is cost-effective and allows for a comprehensive understanding of ancient Rome's most iconic sites.

Location: Via della Salara Vecchia, 5/6, 00186 Roma

Website: www.coopculture.it/en/poi/roman-forum-and-palatine/

TREVI FOUNTAIN

The Trevi Fountain, a jewel of Baroque architecture, is not only Rome's largest but also its most famous fountain. Completed in 1762 and designed by Nicola Salvi, the fountain is a grandiose display of sculptural art, featuring the majestic figure of Neptune, god of the sea, flanked by two Tritons. The intricate composition of mythical figures and cascading water against the façade of Palazzo Poli creates a mesmerizing spectacle. According to enduring tradition, tossing a coin into the fountain over your left shoulder with your right hand ensures a return to Rome. The fountain's allure extends beyond its architectural grandeur; it symbolizes the romance and legends of the Eternal City, captivating visitors from around the globe.

Tip: To fully appreciate the fountain's beauty without the crowds, plan to visit early in the morning or late at night. These quieter moments offer a more intimate experience with the monument. Besides the coin-throwing ritual, take time to admire the artistry of the sculptures and the vibrant play of light on the water. A visit to the Trevi Fountain is not just a visual delight but a chance to partake in a time-honored Roman tradition, making it an essential stop in any Roman itinerary.

Location: Piazza di Trevi, 00187 Roma RM, Italy
Website: www.turismoroma.it/en/places/trevi-fountain

SPANISH STEPS

The Spanish Steps, an iconic symbol of Roman Baroque architecture, gracefully cascade from the Piazza di Spagna to the Piazza Trinità dei Monti. Built in the 18th century and consisting of 135 steps, this monumental stairway is a masterpiece that reflects the artistic and cultural flourishes of its era. The Trinità dei Monti church, perched majestically at the top, adds a touch of elegance to the already picturesque scene. The steps have long been a favorite gathering place for locals and tourists alike, offering a splendid vantage point to observe the lively buzz of the city. In the spring, the steps are adorned with vibrant azaleas, enhancing their beauty and making them a photographer's delight. The area around the Spanish Steps, including the Piazza di Spagna with its Barcaccia Fountain and the upscale shopping street of Via dei Condotti, is a hive of activity, brimming with chic boutiques, cafes, and street artists.

Tip: While the steps are a perfect spot for relaxation and people-watching, visitors are encouraged to be mindful of the local regulations regarding sitting and eating on the steps to preserve their historical integrity. Early mornings or evenings offer a more serene experience, away from the midday crowds. The nearby streets also offer a variety of dining and shopping options, making the area around the Spanish Steps a comprehensive cultural and leisure experience. During the Christmas season the area takes on a festive atmosphere, with beautiful lights and decorations, adding to its charm.

Location: Piazza di Spagna, 00187 Roma RM, Italy

Website: www.turismoroma.it/en/places/spanish-steps

ST. PETER'S BASILICA

St. Peter's Basilica, standing majestically in Vatican City, is not only a pivotal site of religious significance but also a masterpiece of Renaissance architecture. Commissioned by Pope Julius II and featuring contributions from legendary architects like Michelangelo and Bernini, the basilica is a testament to artistic and architectural grandeur. Its iconic dome is a prominent feature of the Roman skyline, drawing visitors from across the globe. The interior of the basilica is equally magnificent, with awe-inspiring artworks including Michelangelo's Pietà, Bernini's Baldachin, and the opulent Papal Altar. The basilica also claims to house the tomb of St. Peter, one of the twelve apostles of Jesus and the first Bishop of Rome, making it a site of profound historical and spiritual importance. The expansive nave, intricate mosaics, and lavishly decorated chapels and altars inside the basilica create an atmosphere of reverence and beauty, embodying the essence of Catholic tradition and art.

Tip: While entrance to the basilica is free, it is advisable to arrive early to avoid long queues, especially during peak tourist seasons. Visitors should dress respectfully, covering shoulders and knees, as it is a place of worship. For those willing to ascend to the dome, the climb offers a breathtaking panoramic view of Rome and the Vatican. There is a fee for the dome climb, and visitors can choose between taking the stairs or the elevator for the initial

part of the ascent. The visit to the dome is a must-do for its unparalleled vistas and the up-close view of the basilica's impressive architecture.

Location: Piazza San Pietro, 00120 Città del Vaticano,
Website: www.basilicasanpietro.va/en.html

SISTINE CHAPEL

The Sistine Chapel, a jewel within the Vatican Museums, is renowned for Michelangelo's extraordinary frescoes. The most famous of these are the ceiling frescoes, including the iconic 'Creation of Adam', and 'The Last Judgment' on the altar wall. Painted between 1508 and 1512, the ceiling depicts scenes from Genesis and is considered one of the greatest masterpieces of Renaissance art. 'The Last Judgment,' created later in Michelangelo's life, is a powerful and moving depiction of the second coming of Christ. The chapel's walls also feature works by other celebrated Renaissance artists like Botticelli and Perugino. Beyond its artistic significance, the Sistine Chapel holds immense religious importance as the site of the Papal Conclave, where new popes are elected in a centuries-old tradition. A visit to the Sistine Chapel is an opportunity to immerse oneself in a space that intertwines sublime artistry with deep spiritual significance, offering an experience that resonates far beyond its walls.

Tip: To avoid long queues, it is advisable to book tickets to the Vatican Museums, which include entry to the Sistine Chapel, in advance. Note that photography is not permitted inside, and visitors are expected to maintain silence. Dress respectfully, covering shoulders and knees. For a less crowded visit, early morning or late afternoon times are recommended.

Location: 00120 Vatican City

Website:
www.museivaticani.va/content/museivaticani/en/collezioni/musei/cappella-sistina/storia-cappella-sistina.html

PIAZZA NAVONA

Piazza Navona, a masterpiece of Baroque Rome, is one of the city's most picturesque and vibrant squares. Built on the site of the ancient Stadium of Domitian, it retains the shape of the original racetrack. The square is dominated by three magnificent fountains: the central and most famous being Bernini's Fountain of the Four Rivers (Fontana dei Quattro Fiumi), a symbolic representation of the world's major rivers across four continents. Flanking it are the Fountain of Neptune and the Moor Fountain. Another architectural highlight is the Church of Sant'Agnese in Agone, designed by Borromini, Bernini's rival, adding to the square's artistic and historical richness. Today, Piazza Navona is a bustling hub, surrounded by restaurants, cafes, and street artists, making it a lively spot for both locals and tourists. The baroque buildings that line the piazza add to its charm and grandeur, making it a quintessential Roman experience.

Tip: The square is an ideal location for people-watching and enjoying the lively atmosphere of the city. Grab a gelato from a nearby shop and take a leisurely stroll around the square to admire its artistic and architectural beauty. Visiting during Christmas provides an added charm, as the square hosts a festive market and becomes adorned with holiday decorations and lights. It's also a great spot to enjoy an evening out, as the fountains are beautifully illuminated after dark, adding to the magical ambiance of the square.

Location: Piazza Navona, 00186 Roma RM, Italy

Website: www.turismoroma.it/en/places/navona-square

VILLA BORGHESE

Villa Borghese, Rome's third-largest public park, is a verdant oasis in the heart of the bustling city. This expansive landscape garden, designed in the naturalistic English manner, offers a serene and picturesque environment, featuring meandering paths, tranquil water features, and diverse flora. At its heart lies the Borghese Gallery (Galleria Borghese), a treasure trove of art housing masterpieces by renowned artists like Caravaggio, Bernini, and Titian, set within a magnificent 17th-century villa. The park also includes other cultural institutions like the Etruscan Museum, the Casa del Cinema, and the Rome Zoo (Bioparco di Roma), making it a multifaceted destination for art, culture, and nature enthusiasts. Whether for jogging, picnicking, boating on its small lake, or simply enjoying a leisurely stroll amidst its scenic beauty, Villa Borghese provides a delightful escape from the urban landscape of Rome.

Tip: To visit the Borghese Gallery, booking a timed entrance ticket in advance is highly recommended, as the museum limits the number of visitors to preserve the intimate experience. The park itself is perfect for leisure activities – consider renting a bike or a rowboat to explore its vastness. For those interested in a more in-depth cultural experience, the park's other museums offer a variety of exhibitions and collections. The Pincio Terrace, located near the park, provides one of the best views of Rome, making it a perfect spot for sunset viewing.

Location: Piazzale Napoleone I, 00197 Roma RM, Italy

Website: www.turismoroma.it/en/places/villa-borghese-park

CASTEL SANT'ANGELO

Castel Sant'Angelo, a striking cylindrical building along the banks of the Tiber River, is steeped in the history of Rome. Originally constructed as a mausoleum for Emperor Hadrian and his family, this remarkable structure has transformed over centuries, serving as a fortress, a papal residence, and now a museum. The castle is famed for its Passetto di Borgo, a secret passageway that once allowed popes to flee to safety in times of danger. Its rich history is palpable in its layered architecture, which chronicles Rome's evolution from antiquity to the Renaissance. The museum inside showcases an array of sculptures, paintings, and military memorabilia. Visitors can explore various rooms, including the papal apartments, and enjoy panoramic views of Rome from its terrace. The view from Castel Sant'Angelo offers a breathtaking vista encompassing the Vatican, the Tiber River, and beyond, particularly enchanting at sunset when the city is bathed in golden hues.

Tip: Visiting Castel Sant'Angelo in the late afternoon allows you to experience the changing light over Rome, culminating in a stunning sunset view from the top. The castle frequently hosts temporary exhibitions and cultural events, so check their schedule for any special activities during your visit. For a comprehensive experience, consider a guided tour to fully understand the historical significance of this multifaceted monument.

The bridge leading to the castle, Ponte Sant'Angelo, lined with angelic sculptures, is also worth a leisurely stroll for its scenic and historical value.

Location: Lungotevere Castello, 50, 00193 Roma RM, Italy

Website: www.castelsantangelo.com

CAPITOLINE HILL

Capitoline Hill, the smallest yet most significant of Rome's seven hills, has played a central role in the city's history since ancient times. It was once the religious and political heart of Rome, and today, it continues to be a hub of cultural and historical importance. The hill is home to the Capitoline Museums (Musei Capitolini), a treasure trove of classical sculpture and Renaissance art. These museums, housed in two palatial buildings surrounding the Michelangelo-designed Piazza del Campidoglio, contain an extensive collection of ancient Roman statues, inscriptions, and artifacts, alongside paintings and sculptures from later periods. The piazza itself, with its geometric design and the replica statue of Marcus Aurelius at its center, is a masterpiece of Renaissance urban planning. The panoramic view from the hill overlooks the Roman Forum and the Colosseum, offering a visual connection to the city's ancient past. Visiting Capitoline Hill provides not only an opportunity to delve into Rome's rich history but also to appreciate the architectural innovations that have shaped the cityscape.

Tip: Dedicate ample time to explore both museums and the piazza, as the collections are extensive. The terrace of the Tabularium, accessible from inside the museum, provides one of the best views of the Roman Forum. The Caffè Capitolino, located on the museum premises, is a perfect spot to relax and enjoy a meal or a coffee with a view. Consider visiting late in the afternoon when the crowd thins out, offering a more tranquil experience of the museums and the piazza.

Location: Piazza del Campidoglio, 00186 Roma RM, Italy

Website: www.turismoroma.it/en/page/capitoline-hill-place-legends

HIDDEN GEMS AND LESSER-KNOWN SIGHTS IN ROME

TRASTEVERE

Trastevere is a picturesque and historic neighborhood in Rome, known for its narrow, winding cobblestone streets and distinctive medieval charm. This area, with its ivy-clad buildings and vibrant atmosphere, offers a delightful escape from the more crowded tourist locales. Trastevere is a hub of local life, boasting an array of traditional trattorias, quaint cafes, and unique artisan shops. The neighborhood is anchored by the Piazza di Santa Maria and the Basilica of Santa Maria in Trastevere, one of Rome's oldest churches, renowned for its stunning mosaics. As the sun sets, Trastevere's streets come alive with a lively dining and nightlife scene, with restaurants and bars spilling out onto the streets, creating an inviting atmosphere for locals and visitors alike. This district perfectly encapsulates the Roman lifestyle, blending historical beauty with a contemporary, bohemian spirit.

Tip: Venture into the lesser-trodden alleys of Trastevere to discover its hidden gems, from charming boutiques to cozy local eateries. The area is particularly enchanting in the evening when the streets are bathed in golden light and the vibrant social life of the neighborhood is most evident. Enjoying a meal or a drink in one of the many outdoor settings

here offers an authentic taste of Roman life.

Location: Trastevere, Rome, Italy

Website: www.turismoroma.it/en/page/unusual-trastevere

GALLERIA BORGHESE

Nestled within the verdant landscape of Villa Borghese, the Galleria Borghese is a true hidden gem in Rome, often overshadowed by the city's larger museums. This 17th-century villa houses an exquisite collection of art that includes sculptures, antiquities, and paintings, making it a paradise for art enthusiasts. The gallery's highlights are its stunning sculptures by Gian Lorenzo Bernini, capturing the artist's mastery of marble, and captivating paintings by Caravaggio, showcasing his dramatic use of light and shadow. Works by Raphael add to the gallery's allure, offering glimpses into the Renaissance genius. The villa itself is an architectural marvel, with its opulent decor and beautifully manicured gardens, providing a tranquil retreat from the city's hustle. The Galleria Borghese not only presents some of the finest art in Rome but also offers an intimate, uncrowded atmosphere, allowing visitors to truly immerse themselves in the beauty of each masterpiece.

Tip: Due to its popularity and limited capacity, booking tickets in advance is essential. Visitors are given a fixed time slot, typically two hours, to explore the gallery, ensuring a relaxed and uncrowded experience. The gallery's location within Villa Borghese makes it ideal for combining an art visit with a leisurely stroll or picnic in the surrounding gardens. The Galleria Borghese is smaller than other major museums in Rome, making it manageable and particularly enjoyable for those seeking a more intimate art experience.

Location: Piazzale Scipione Borghese, 5, 00197 Roma RM,

Website: www.borghese.gallery

Campo de' Fiori, a quintessential Roman square, offers a unique blend of historical charm and vibrant daily life. By day, it hosts one of Rome's most famous and traditional markets, bustling with vendors selling fresh fruits, vegetables, flowers, and an array of local specialties. The market, steeped in history, has been a focal point of Roman life for centuries, providing a lively and colorful glimpse into the city's culinary culture. As the sun sets, the square seamlessly transitions into a lively nightlife hub, surrounded by an eclectic mix of bars, restaurants, and cafes. It becomes a popular gathering place for both locals and visitors, drawn to its energetic atmosphere and the chance to savor authentic Roman cuisine or enjoy a classic Italian aperitivo. The square's history is also marked by the statue of the philosopher Giordano Bruno, a reminder of its past as a site of public executions.

Tip: To fully experience the market's vibrancy, plan to visit in the morning when the stalls are brimming with fresh produce and local delicacies. The evenings offer a different charm, ideal for enjoying a drink and people-watching in one of the lively establishments surrounding the square. Dining al fresco here provides a perfect opportunity to soak in the ambiance of Roman nightlife. The square is also a great starting point to explore the surrounding streets of the

historic center, which are rich in history and character.
Location: Piazza Campo de' Fiori, 00186 Roma RM
Website: www.turismoroma.it/en/places/campo-de'-fiori-and-piazza-farnese

PALATINE HILL

Palatine Hill, one of the seven hills of Rome, is steeped in myth and history, offering a unique perspective on the city's ancient past. According to legend, it is the site where the she-wolf discovered the infant twins Romulus and Remus, the founders of Rome. This hill, overlooking the Roman Forum and the Circus Maximus, is a treasure trove of archaeological significance. Visitors can explore the remnants of grand imperial palaces, including the Flavian Palace and the House of Augustus, adorned with beautiful frescoes. The ruins, set amidst lush gardens and towering pine trees, evoke a sense of the hill's former glory and importance. The Palatine also offers some of the best panoramic views of Rome, encompassing the Colosseum, the Roman Forum, and the modern cityscape. A visit here is a journey back in time, walking through the same paths that ancient Romans once tread, surrounded by the echoes of history.

Tip: Comfortable footwear is essential, as the site involves a fair amount of walking on uneven terrain. A combined ticket, which includes access to the Colosseum, Roman Forum, and Palatine Hill, is a cost-effective way to explore these interconnected historical sites. Allocate sufficient time to wander through the extensive grounds and soak in the hill's historical and natural beauty. Early morning or late afternoon visits can offer a more tranquil experience and a chance to see the ruins bathed in the soft light of the golden hour.

Location: Palatine Hill 00186 Rome, RM, Italy

Website: www.coopculture.it/it/poi/foro-romano-e-palatino

The Basilica of Santa Maria Maggiore, one of the four major basilicas in Rome, is a magnificent testament to religious art and architecture. Distinguished by its blend of classical, medieval, and baroque elements, the basilica stands as a beacon of historical and artistic significance. It is renowned for its stunning 5th-century mosaics, which adorn the nave and triumphal arch, depicting scenes from the Old Testament and the life of Christ. These mosaics are among the oldest representations of the Virgin Mary in Christian art. The basilica also houses the Salus Populi Romani, a highly venerated Marian icon, believed to have miraculous properties. The interior is equally impressive, with a richly gilded coffered ceiling and exquisite Cosmatesque floors. Another highlight is the Sistine Chapel, not to be mistaken for its more famous counterpart in the Vatican, which contains the tomb of Pope Sixtus V. The Borghese Chapel, with its opulent decorations, is another must-see within the basilica.

Tip: Santa Maria Maggiore offers a serene and less crowded atmosphere compared to other major basilicas in Rome, making it ideal for visitors seeking a more contemplative experience. Take time to explore the various chapels and artworks within the basilica, each with its own story and artistic merit. The basilica is open daily, and entry is free, although respectful attire is required. The tranquility of the basilica provides a perfect

setting to appreciate the intricate details of its mosaics and the artistic heritage it embodies.

Location: P.za di Santa Maria Maggiore, 00100 Roma RM,

Website: www.basilicasantamariamaggiore.va/en.html

The Circus Maximus, a vast valley between the Aventine and Palatine Hills, is steeped in the history of ancient Roman entertainment. Once the premier chariot racing stadium and mass entertainment venue of Rome, it could accommodate over 250,000 spectators in its heyday. While much of its original structure has given way to time, the elongated oval track and the imagination of visitors keep the spirit of the races alive. Today, it serves as a public park, offering a serene and open space for leisurely strolls, jogging, and picnics, with splendid views of the surrounding historical landmarks, especially the Palatine Hill. The area also becomes a lively hub for major concerts and public events, drawing crowds for a different kind of spectacle. Walking through the Circus Maximus, one can envision the thrilling chariot races, the roars of the ancient crowds, and the dynamic atmosphere that once defined this iconic Roman site.

Tip: For a peaceful visit, consider exploring the Circus Maximus early in the morning or during sunset when the area is less crowded and the lighting is particularly beautiful. The site occasionally hosts temporary exhibitions, historical reenactments, and cultural events, offering visitors a chance to experience a blend of modern entertainment and historical ambiance. Check the local schedule for any special events during your visit. The vast open space of the Circus Maximus is also ideal for those interested in Roman history and provides a unique perspective on the city's ancient past.

Location: Via del Circo Massimo, 00186 Roma RM, Italy

Website: www.turismoroma.it/en/places/circus-maximus

The Aventine Keyhole, an unassuming yet enchanting spot located on the Aventine Hill, offers one of Rome's most unique and charming views. This small keyhole, part of the gate to the Priory of the Knights of Malta, perfectly frames a distant view of St. Peter's Basilica, creating a remarkable visual alignment that leaves visitors in awe. The keyhole presents a picturesque vista that encapsulates the essence of Rome's beauty and mystery. The experience of peeking through this keyhole is like looking into another world – a perfectly composed image of the iconic basilica set against lush garden greenery. The Aventine Hill itself is a serene and picturesque area, away from the bustling city center, and is known for its beautiful churches, gardens, and orange trees. The keyhole's allure lies in its simplicity and the surprise element of discovering such a captivating view through an ordinary gate.

Tip: The best time to visit the Aventine Keyhole is during the day when the basilica is clearly visible in the distance. The area around the keyhole is usually quiet, making it a peaceful escape from the city's busier tourist spots. After enjoying this unique view, visitors can explore the nearby Garden of Oranges (Giardino degli Aranci) for panoramic views of Rome and a tranquil setting. The Aventine Hill itself is worth exploring, with its historic churches and quiet streets that offer a glimpse into a lesser-known side of Rome.

Location: Piazza dei Cavalieri di Malta, 00153 Roma RM

Website: www.turismoroma.it/en/places/villa-magistrale-sovereign-order-malta-aventine

MOUTH OF TRUTH (BOCCA DELLA VERITÀ)

The Mouth of Truth, or "Bocca della Verità," is an intriguing and iconic marble mask that has captured the imaginations of visitors to Rome for generations. Housed in the portico of the Church of Santa Maria in Cosmedin, this large, circular stone face is steeped in legend and mystery. According to popular belief, the Mouth of Truth will bite off the hand of anyone who tells a lie while their hand is placed in its mouth. This legend has turned the Mouth of Truth into a favorite spot for tourists seeking to test their honesty. The origin of the mask is uncertain; it dates back to the 1st century AD and is thought to have been part of a Roman fountain or a manhole cover. Its enigmatic expression and the folklore surrounding it make it a unique and memorable part of Rome's rich tapestry of history and myth.

Tip: The Mouth of Truth is a popular attraction, often resulting in long queues for a chance to take a photo. To avoid the crowds, try to visit early in the morning. The site is not only a fun stop for a quirky photo opportunity but also a chance to explore the beautiful Church of Santa Maria in Cosmedin, a fine example of medieval architecture, and the nearby area, which is rich in history and less frequented by tourists. The nearby Tiber River and the ancient Forum Boarium also offer additional historical sights worth exploring.

Location: Piazza della Bocca della Verità, 18, 00186 Roma RM, Italy

Website: www.turismoroma.it/en/places/mouth-truth

Santa Maria in Trastevere is one of the oldest and most beloved churches in Rome, nestled in the heart of the vibrant Trastevere neighborhood. Dating back to the early Christian era, the church has been rebuilt and embellished over the centuries, most notably in the 12th and 13th centuries when the stunning golden mosaics were added. These mosaics, depicting biblical scenes and saints, shimmer beautifully under the church's lights, creating an atmosphere of tranquility and reverence. The façade of the church, with its distinctive medieval bell tower, is a prominent feature in the bustling Piazza di Santa Maria in Trastevere. The interior of the church, apart from its spectacular mosaics, features ancient columns taken from Roman baths and temples, and a coffered ceiling that adds to its historical and artistic charm. The church's serene ambiance provides a stark contrast to the lively atmosphere of the surrounding piazza and neighborhood, known for its lively dining and nightlife scene.

Tip: The church and the surrounding piazza take on a magical quality in the evening when illuminated. It's a perfect time to visit for both the spiritual atmosphere inside the church and the lively social scene outside. After exploring the church, enjoy a stroll in the neighborhood to experience the charming streets of Trastevere and its array of restaurants and cafes. The church often hosts classical music concerts and other cultural events,

so check the schedule for any special happenings during your visit.

Location: Piazza di Santa Maria in Trastevere, 00153 Roma

Website: www.santamariaintrastevere.it

PARKS AND GARDENS
IN ROME
VILLA ADA

Villa Ada, once a royal residence and now one of Rome's largest public parks, offers a peaceful escape from the city's hustle. This expansive green space is a treasure trove of natural beauty, featuring diverse flora, tranquil pathways, and a serene lake. Its vast area allows for a variety of recreational activities, including jogging, cycling, and horseback riding, making it a popular destination for both locals and visitors seeking outdoor relaxation and exercise. The park's undulating landscape and dense vegetation create a sense of seclusion and tranquility, ideal for those looking to immerse themselves in nature. Villa Ada is not only a haven for outdoor enthusiasts but also a cultural hotspot. During the summer months, it becomes a vibrant venue for music concerts, festivals, and cultural events, drawing crowds for open-air entertainment amidst its picturesque setting.

Tip: To truly appreciate the park's natural beauty, venture along its less frequented trails. These quieter paths offer a perfect opportunity for bird watching and discovering the park's hidden corners. The park's size makes it ideal for long, leisurely walks or picnics. For those interested in Rome's history, the park also contains some historical buildings and ruins, adding an element of intrigue to your visit.

Location: Via Salaria, 267, 273/275 Roma RM, Italy

Website: www.turismoroma.it/en/places/villa-ada-savoia

THE GARDENS OF THE VATICAN

The Vatican Gardens, a splendid oasis within the Vatican City, offer a serene and picturesque retreat from the bustling streets of Rome. Covering approximately half of the Vatican's territory, these meticulously maintained gardens are a testament to the artistic and horticultural traditions of the Renaissance and Baroque periods. The gardens are adorned with a diverse array of flora, elegantly designed flowerbeds, ornamental fountains, and sculptures, creating a tranquil and meditative environment. In addition to their natural beauty, the gardens are rich in history, featuring medieval fortifications, various monuments, and intricate walkways. Visitors can also view the Vatican Radio's headquarters nestled within the gardens. The harmonious blend of art, nature, and spirituality in the Vatican Gardens makes them a unique and peaceful haven, reflecting the centuries-old heritage of the Vatican.

Tip: Visiting the Vatican Gardens requires joining a guided tour, which often includes access to the Vatican Museums. As these tours are in high demand and visitor numbers are limited, it's crucial to book well in advance. The guided tour provides not only an opportunity to explore these exquisite gardens but also insights into their history, significance, and the various artworks and structures within them. The peaceful ambiance of the gardens offers a stark contrast to the more crowded areas of the Vatican, making it a uniquely calming experience. The tour duration varies, so ensure you have ample time to enjoy both the gardens and the museums.

Location: Via Paolo VI, 29, 00120 Città del Vaticano, Vatican City
Website: www.museivaticani.va/content/museivaticani/en.html

VILLA DORIA PAMPHILI

Villa Doria Pamphili, the largest public park in Rome, is a magnificent example of Italian Baroque garden design, offering a tranquil escape from the urban hustle. This sprawling green haven is characterized by its expansive manicured lawns, elegantly designed fountains, and a variety of trees and plants, creating a serene and picturesque setting. Winding pathways and secluded spots invite visitors for peaceful walks, jogs, or leisurely picnics. The centerpiece of the park is the majestic Villa Doria Pamphili, a historic estate that enhances the park's beauty and grandeur. The villa's façade, overlooking the lush gardens, reflects the architectural elegance of the Baroque era. The park's diverse landscape also includes a small lake, making it a habitat for various bird species, adding to its natural charm. Its vast size and diverse features make Villa Doria Pamphili a popular destination for both relaxation and outdoor activities, away from the city's more frequented tourist spots.

Tip: The park's extensive area and relatively fewer crowds make it an ideal spot for those seeking a quiet and relaxing environment. It's perfect for a morning jog, an afternoon picnic, or a leisurely stroll at sunset. The varied landscape, with its open fields and shaded areas, caters to different preferences, whether you're looking to bask in the sun or find a cool retreat under the trees. Art and history enthusiasts may also enjoy exploring the architectural details of the villa and its surroundings. Additionally, the park hosts occasional cultural events and exhibitions, adding to its appeal as a destination that combines nature, art, and leisure.

Location: Via di S. Pancrazio, 00152 Roma RM, Italy

Website: www.villadoriapamphilj.it

THE ORANGE GARDEN

Known in Italian as 'Parco Savello', the Orange Garden is a quaint, picturesque garden located on the Aventine Hill. Famous for its orange trees, this park offers one of the most stunning views of Rome, overlooking the Tiber and several iconic landmarks. It's an ideal spot for a romantic stroll or a peaceful break amidst the beauty of nature.

Tip: Visit at sunset for a breathtaking view of Rome. The keyhole view of St. Peter's Basilica through the Knights of Malta's gateway nearby is a must-see.

Location: Piazza Pietro D'Illiria, 00153 Roma RM, Italy

Website: www.turismoroma.it/en/places/savello-park-or-orange-garden

ROSETO COMUNALE

The Roseto Comunale, or the Municipal Rose Garden, is a botanical garden located on Rome's Aventine Hill. This enchanting garden, overlooking the Circus Maximus, is home to over 1,100 varieties of roses from all over the world. The garden's layout symbolically traces the path of the ancient Jewish cemetery that once occupied the site.

Tip: The best time to visit is during May when the roses are in full bloom. Entrance is free, making it a lovely, budget-friendly stop in Rome.

Location: Via di Valle Murcia, 6 Clivo dei Publicii, 3, Roma RM, Italy

Website: www.turismoroma.it/en/places/rose-garden

ROME'S CULINARY SCENE

LA PERGOLA

La Pergola, Rome's first and only three-Michelin-star restaurant, offers a gourmet dining experience. Led by celebrated chef Heinz Beck, this restaurant is known for its innovative Italian cuisine, exceptional wine list, and stunning views of the Eternal City.

Tip: Reservations are essential and should be made well in advance. Dress code is formal, adding to the exclusivity of the experience.

Location: Via Alberto Cadlolo, 101, 00136 Roma RM, Italy

Website: www.romecavalieri.com/la-pergola/

TRATTORIA VECCHIA ROMA

Trattoria Vecchia Roma is a beloved eatery offering a genuine Roman dining experience. Known for its traditional Roman cuisine, it specializes in classic dishes like 'Amatriciana' and 'Carbonara,' served authentically and heartily. The cozy trattoria is celebrated for its pasta dishes, notably served in a Parmesan cheese wheel, a treat for both the eyes and the palate.

Tip: Booking in advance is recommended due to its popularity. Don't miss the opportunity to enjoy their signature pasta dishes for an authentic Roman culinary experience.

Location: Via Ferruccio, 12/b/c, 00185 Roma RM, Italy

Website: www.trattoriavecchiaroma.it

PIZZARIUM BONCI

Pizzarium Bonci, led by acclaimed baker Gabriele Bonci, has redefined pizza al taglio (pizza by the slice) in Rome. Known for inventive toppings and impeccable quality, each slice features a perfectly crispy crust and fresh, seasonal ingredients. This modest shop has garnered a cult following for its unique take on a classic Roman staple. Visitors are treated

to an ever-changing menu, making each visit a new culinary discovery.
Tip: Anticipate queues, but the diverse, delicious slices are well worth

the wait. Sampling various options offers a taste of Bonci's creativity.
Location: Via della Meloria, 43, 00136 Roma RM, Italy
Website: www.bonci.it/en/bonci/

FELICE A TESTACCIO

In the lively Testaccio neighborhood lies Felice a Testaccio, an iconic restaurant celebrated for its authentic Roman cuisine. The eatery is especially renowned for its Cacio e Pepe, a dish that exemplifies the simplicity and richness of Roman flavors. The ambiance combines tradition with a bustling Roman atmosphere, making it a favorite among locals and tourists. The menu offers a range of classic Roman dishes, each prepared with a commitment to authenticity and quality.

Tip: Reservations are recommended to secure a table in this popular spot. Don't miss their Tiramisu for a delightful end to your meal.
Location: Via Mastro Giorgio, 29, 00153 Roma RM, Italy

Website: www.feliceatestacci o.com/#

PASTA CARBONARA

Pasta Carbonara is a hallmark of Roman cuisine, celebrated for its creamy texture and rich flavor. Traditionally prepared with eggs, Pecorino Romano cheese, guanciale, and black pepper, this dish exemplifies culinary simplicity and excellence. It's a staple in Roman trattorias, where mastery in blending these humble ingredients is key. Carbonara, known for its absence of cream, is a must-try for its authentic Roman taste.

Where to Try: Experience genuine Carbonara at "Roscioli Salumeria con Cucina." **Location** for Roscioli: Via dei Giubbonari, 21, 00186 Roma RM, Italy. **Tip**: Seek places that stick to the traditional recipe, avoiding any addition of cream or milk.

SALTIMBOCCA

Saltimbocca, literally translating to "jumps in the mouth," is a classic Roman dish that perfectly captures the essence of Italian cooking. It consists of tender veal escalopes, topped with a slice of salty prosciutto and an aromatic sage leaf, often secured with a toothpick. The veal is lightly marinated in wine, which adds depth to the dish's flavor. When cooked, Saltimbocca offers a harmonious blend of meaty, herby, and salty tastes, embodying the simplicity yet sophistication of Roman cuisine. **Where to Try**: "Hostaria Romana" is acclaimed for serving one of Rome's finest Saltimbocca. **Location** for Hostaria Romana: Via del Boccaccio, 1, 00187 Roma RM, Italy **Tip**: For an authentic Roman dining experience, pair Saltimbocca with classic Roman sides like roasted potatoes or a crisp salad. This combination balances the flavors and textures, making for a truly delightful meal.

SUPPLÌ

Supplì are a Roman culinary delight, consisting of fried rice balls traditionally filled with tomato sauce, mozzarella, and occasionally minced meat. These snacks, crispy on the outside and gooey inside, epitomize Roman street food. Supplì offer a burst of flavors and textures, showcasing the simplicity and richness of local cuisine. Often served as a quick snack or appetizer, they're a must-try for a genuine taste of Rome.

Where to Try: "Supplizio" in Rome is renowned for its variety of supplì.
Location for Supplizio: Via dei Banchi Vecchi, 143, 00186 Roma RM, Italy
Tip: Best enjoyed hot, supplì are perfect for on-the-go eating while exploring the city.

GELATO

Gelato is Italy's artisanal answer to ice cream, renowned for its rich texture and intense flavors. In Rome, gelaterias excel in creating this delightful dessert, offering both traditional and innovative flavors. Unlike regular ice cream, gelato is made with a higher proportion of milk, less cream, and no egg yolks, resulting in a denser and more flavorful experience. Rome's gelato is a culinary art form, often prepared with fresh, high-quality ingredients and a variety of natural flavors ranging from fruits to nuts. Each serving is a testament to Italy's passion for fine food and flavor.

Where to Try: "Giolitti," one of Rome's oldest and most esteemed gelaterias.
Location for Giolitti: Via Uffici del Vicario, 40, 00186 Roma RM, Italy
Tip: Gelaterias typically allow tastings, so don't hesitate to sample different flavors. Local favorites like pistachio and hazelnut are a must-try for an authentic Roman gelato experience.

TIRAMISU

Tiramisu, a renowned Italian dessert, has found a special place in Rome's culinary heart. Comprising layers of coffee-soaked ladyfingers and a fluffy blend of eggs, sugar, and mascarpone cheese, it's finished with a dusting of cocoa. This indulgent dessert, originating from Veneto, is a staple in Roman cafes and restaurants. Each layer of Tiramisu offers a rich and velvety texture, combined with the invigorating flavor of coffee, creating a perfectly balanced and irresistible treat. Its name, translating to "pick me up," aptly describes the delightful experience it offers. **Where to Try**: "Pompi" is celebrated in Rome for its exquisite Tiramisu. **Location** for Pompi: Via Albalonga, 7 Piazza Re di Roma, 00183 Roma RM, Italy. **Tip**: Savor Tiramisu in a Roman cafe as an exquisite end to your meal, ideally paired with a robust espresso. This dessert is a quintessential Roman experience, blending tradition with culinary artistry.

FRASCATI WINE

Frascati Wine, with its origins in the verdant hills of the Roman countryside, is a celebrated white wine, cherished for its crisp and refreshing quality. Made predominantly from Malvasia and Trebbiano grapes, it offers a light, aromatic profile that complements the flavors of Roman cuisine perfectly. This wine is a fixture in the city's culinary scene, served in bars and restaurants across Rome. Its versatility makes it an excellent choice for a variety of dishes, from antipasti to seafood. **Where to Try**: "Enoteca Ferrara" in Rome provides an excellent selection of Frascati Wine. **Location** for Enoteca Ferrara: Piazza Trilussa, 41, 00153 Roma RM, Italy. **Tip**: Embark on a journey to the Frascati vineyards just outside Rome for an authentic wine-tasting experience. This excursion offers not only a taste of the wine but also insights into its traditional production methods and the region's rich viticultural history.

SHOPPING IN ROME

VIA DEL CORSO

Via del Corso is a vibrant main shopping street in Rome, stretching from Piazza Venezia to Piazza del Popolo. Renowned for its eclectic mix of high-street fashion brands and charming boutiques, it's a haven for shoppers of all kinds. The bustling avenue is perfect for those seeking the latest trends or unique finds. Amidst the historic ambiance of Rome, Via del Corso offers a modern shopping experience, making it a must-visit destination for fashion enthusiasts and casual shoppers.

Tip: For a more relaxed experience, consider visiting on weekday mornings to avoid the weekend crowds.
Location: Via del Corso, Rome, Italy
Website: www.turismoroma.it/en/places/del-corso

VIA CONDOTTI

Via Condotti, located near the Spanish Steps, is Rome's most illustrious shopping street. This elegant avenue is lined with luxury boutiques from world-famous brands like Gucci, Prada, and Bulgari. Renowned for its upscale atmosphere and historic architecture, Via Condotti is not only a shopper's paradise but also a picturesque destination for window shopping and experiencing the epitome of Italian fashion.

Tip: Even if luxury shopping isn't your plan, Via Condotti offers a delightful experience with its chic ambiance and historic charm. Strolling along this street is ideal for soaking in the sophisticated side of Rome.

Location: Via dei Condotti, Rome, Italy
Website:www.turismoroma.it/en/page/shopping-streets

MERCATO MONTI

Mercato Monti, nestled in Rome's hip Monti district, is a haven for fashion enthusiasts and treasure hunters. This urban market, bustling with activity, features an array of stalls selling vintage clothing, handmade accessories, and unique artisanal crafts. It's a popular spot among Rome's young and stylish crowd, offering a diverse range of one-of-a-kind items and local designs. The market's vibrant atmosphere makes it a must-visit for anyone looking to explore Rome's contemporary fashion and artistic scene.

Tip: Open mainly on weekends, it's the perfect place to find distinctive souvenirs and support emerging local designers and artists.

Location: Via Baccina, 36, 00184 Roma RM, Italy

Website: www.facebook.com/MercatoMonti

CAMPO DE' FIORI MARKET

Campo de' Fiori Market is one of Rome's oldest and most famous markets, set in a picturesque square. It offers a vibrant atmosphere and a variety of stalls selling fresh produce, flowers, spices, and local delicacies. The market is not only a place to shop but also a window into Roman culture and daily life.

Tip: The market operates in the mornings until around 2:00 PM, Monday to Saturday. It's an excellent spot for purchasing fresh ingredients if you're planning to cook, or simply to enjoy the lively local ambiance.

Location: Campo de' Fiori, 00186 Roma RM, Italy

Website: www.turismoroma.it/en/places/campo-de'-fiori-and-piazza-farnese

GALLERIA ALBERTO SORDI

Galleria Alberto Sordi, set in an exquisite Art Nouveau building in the heart of Rome, is a shopping destination steeped in elegance and history. Originally known as Galleria Colonna, this architectural marvel invites visitors to shop in a setting adorned with intricate mosaics, a stunning glass roof, and ornate decorations. Offering a diverse array of shops, including fashion

boutiques and bookstores, the gallery combines a luxurious shopping experience with architectural beauty. It's a place where shopping intertwines with art, making each visit a delightful and memorable experience.

Location: P.za Colonna, 00187 Roma RM, Italy
Website: www.galleriaalbertosordi.com

PORTA PORTESE FLEA MARKET

Porta Portese, Rome's largest and most renowned flea market, offers a bustling and authentic shopping experience. Every Sunday, its myriad of stalls transform the Trastevere neighborhood into a vibrant marketplace. Here, you can find everything from antiques and vintage clothing to books, records, and unusual curiosities. It's a paradise

for bargain hunters and those seeking unique items with a story. The lively atmosphere, combined with the thrill of discovery, makes Porta Portese a favorite destination for both locals and tourists.

Tip: To snag the best deals and avoid the crowds, arrive early in the morning. Exploring Porta Portese is not just shopping; it's an adventure into the heart of Rome's vibrant street culture.

Location: Piazza di Porta Portese, 00153 Roma RM, Italy
Website: www.turismoroma.it/en/places/mercato-di-porta-portese

BIOPARCO DI ROMA

Bioparco di Roma in Villa Borghese is a captivating zoological garden ideal for family visits. Home to over 200 animal species, it combines education with conservation, making it a perfect place for kids to learn about biodiversity and wildlife protection. The park's engaging environment and interactive exhibits offer a fun and informative experience for all ages.

Tip: Plan to attend the animal feeding sessions and educational talks, which are particularly exciting and educational for children, providing insights into the lives of various species.

Location: Piazzale del, V.le del Giardino Zoologico, 1, 00197 Roma RM, Italy

Website: www.bioparco.it/en

EXPLORA: THE CHILDREN'S MUSEUM

The Children's Museum in Rome is a dynamic space dedicated to interactive learning for young children. With exhibits focusing on science, technology, and the environment, it encourages explorative and hands-on learning. This museum is an excellent destination for families, offering a stimulating environment where children can play, discover, and learn.

Tip: Explora operates on timed entry sessions to manage crowds and enhance the experience. It's recommended to book tickets in advance, especially on weekends, for a smooth and enjoyable visit.

Location: Via Flaminia, 80/86, 00196 Roma RM, Italy

Website: www.mdbr.it/en/

TIME ELEVATOR ROME

Time Elevator Rome is an exhilarating 5D cinema journey through Rome's history. Perfect for families, it combines motion platforms with digital 3D film technology, narrated by Piero Angela. This immersive experience brings Rome's past, from its founding to the Renaissance, to life in a captivating and educational ride. It's a unique way to learn about the city's rich history and a fun activity for children and adults alike.

Tip: Ideal for children aged 4 and above, it's a great educational complement

to visiting Rome's historical sites.
Location: Via dei Santi Apostoli, 20, 00187 Roma RM, Italy
Website: www.time-elevator.it/en/

TECHNOTOWN

Technotown is a futuristic technology and science space located in Villa Torlonia, designed for children and teenagers. It offers interactive experiences that blend learning with fun, featuring activities like virtual reality, robotics, and multimedia installations. It's an excellent venue for stimulating young minds and introducing them to science and technology concepts.

Tip: Technotown is ideal for kids aged 8 and above. Check their program for special workshops and activities, which often change

throughout the year.
Location: Via Lazzaro Spallanzani, 1, 00161 Roma RM, Italy
Website: www.technotown.it

VILLA BORGHESE GARDENS AND PLAYGROUND

Villa Borghese Gardens, one of Rome's largest public parks, is not just a picturesque retreat but also a family-friendly haven. It features a wonderful playground where children can enjoy swings, slides, and various play equipment. The expansive gardens offer ample space for family picnics, leisurely walks, and even boat rides on the charming lake. It's an ideal spot for families to relax and play in a natural setting.

Tip: Consider renting a family-sized pedal cart for a fun and unique way to explore the extensive gardens. Don't miss the opportunity to visit the Bioparco di Roma Zoo, also located within the park, for a complete family outing.

Location: Piazzale Napoleone I, 00197 Roma RM, Italy

Website: www.turismoroma.it/en/places/villa-borghese-park

GLADIATOR SCHOOL

The Gladiator School offers a unique and interactive way to learn about ancient Roman history. Participants, both children and adults, can dress up as gladiators, learn about their weapons and tactics, and even practice some ancient combat techniques in a safe environment. It's an entertaining and educational experience that brings history to life.

experience that brings history to life.

Tip: The school offers various programs, including short introductory lessons and longer, more detailed courses. Booking in advance is recommended, especially during peak tourist seasons.

Location: Via Appia Antica, 18, 00178 Roma RM, Italy

Website: www.gruppostoricoromano.it

ROME BY NIGHT
ILLUMINATED MONUMENTS AND EVENING STROLLS

COLOSSEUM

The Colosseum, an iconic symbol of Ancient Rome, takes on a magical aura at night when it's lit up, creating a dramatic and mesmerizing sight. An evening stroll around the Colosseum offers a different perspective of this ancient amphitheater, with fewer crowds and a more tranquil atmosphere.

Tip: Night tours of the Colosseum are available, providing an exclusive experience to explore the underground chambers and arena floor after dark.

Location: Piazza del Colosseo, 1, 00184 Roma RM, Italy
Website: www.coopculture.it/en/poi/colosseo

TREVI FOUNTAIN

The Trevi Fountain, illuminated at night, is a breathtaking sight. The lights enhance the intricate details of the sculptures and the movement of the water, creating a romantic and enchanting atmosphere. It's a perfect spot for late-night photography or simply to enjoy the beauty of Roman art.

Tip: Tossing a coin into the fountain at night, when it's less crowded, can be a more intimate experience. Enjoy the quieter ambiance away from the daytime hustle.

Location: Piazza di Trevi, 00187 Roma RM, Italy
Website: www.turismoroma.it/en/places/trevi-fountain

PIAZZA NAVONA

Piazza Navona, one of Rome's most famous Baroque squares, is especially charming at night. The fountains, including Bernini's Fountain of the Four Rivers, are beautifully lit, and the vibrant street artists and musicians add to the lively atmosphere. The surrounding bars and restaurants offer a great spot to relax and soak in the ambiance.

Tip: Enjoy a leisurely dinner at one of the piazza's outdoor restaurants for a perfect view of the illuminated fountains and the lively street performances.

Location: Piazza Navona, 00186 Roma RM, Italy

Website: www.turismoroma.it/en/places/navona-square

TRASTEVERE EVENING WALK

Trastevere, with its narrow cobbled streets and medieval architecture, becomes even more enchanting in the evening. The neighborhood is famous for its lively atmosphere, with street musicians, artists, and the warm glow of streetlights reflecting off the old buildings. An evening walk here offers a glimpse into the vibrant local life.

Tip: Don't miss wandering around Piazza di Santa Maria in Trastevere; the church is beautifully lit at night and the piazza is often filled with lively crowds.

Location: Trastevere, Rome, Italy

Website: www.turismoroma.it/en/quartieri/trastevere testaccio

BAR DEL FICO

Bar del Fico, located near Piazza Navona, is a renowned spot in Rome's nightlife, celebrated for its unique bohemian ambiance. This bar is famous for its outdoor seating beneath a sprawling fig tree, creating a picturesque setting. It's a popular choice for both locals and tourists to enjoy an aperitivo or a late-night drink. The bar's vibrant atmosphere

intensifies in the evenings, making it a perfect place to immerse in Rome's lively social scene.

Tip: The best time to visit is during the evening, especially on weekends,

for a lively experience. Bar del Fico is an excellent choice for starting a night out in Rome.
Location: Via della Pace, 34, 00186 Roma RM, Italy
Website: www.bardelfico.com/en/

THE JERRY THOMAS PROJECT

The Jerry Thomas Project is a speakeasy-style cocktail bar, known for its innovative and high-quality drinks. Entrance requires a password (available on their website), adding to the exclusive and mysterious vibe. The bar pays homage to classic mixology, making it a haven for cocktail enthusiasts.

Tip: Make sure to book in advance as the bar is often full. Experiment with their unique cocktails for a memorable experience.

Location: Vicolo Cellini, 30, 00186 Roma RM, Italy
Website: www.thejerrythomasproject.it

FRENI E FRIZIONI

Freni e Frizioni, located in the heart of Trastevere, is a trendy bar known for its lively atmosphere and eclectic crowd. The bar, once a mechanic's workshop, now serves a variety of innovative cocktails and has a large outdoor terrace perfect for socializing on warm nights.

Tip: The bar offers a generous aperitivo buffet in the early evening, making it a great spot to start your night with some drinks and snacks.

Location: Via del Politeama, 4, 00153 Roma RM, Italy

Website: www.freniefrizioni.com/en/

OPEN BALADIN

Open Baladin is a must-visit for beer enthusiasts. Offering an extensive selection of craft beers, both Italian and international, along with a menu of gourmet burgers and other pub fare, it's a favorite among locals and tourists alike. The cozy interior and friendly staff add to the welcoming atmosphere.

Tip: If you're overwhelmed by the beer choices, don't hesitate to ask the knowledgeable staff for recommendations.

Location: Via degli Specchi, 6, 00186 Roma RM, Italy

Website: www.baladin.it/en/

NIGHTCLUBS AND DANCE CLUBS

SHARI VARI PLAYHOUSE

Shari Vari Playhouse, located in the heart of Rome, is a dynamic nightclub known for its diverse music and vibrant atmosphere. This club offers a variety of musical genres throughout the week, ranging from pop to house music, attracting a young and energetic crowd.

Tip: Each night often has a different theme or musical genre, so check their program in advance to choose your preferred night.

Dress to impress as the club has a chic and stylish vibe.
Location: Via de' Nari, 14, 00186 Roma RM, Italy
Website: www.sharivari.it

GOA CLUB

Goa Club is one of Rome's most popular and respected nightclubs, particularly known for electronic and techno music. The club features top-quality sound systems and regularly hosts renowned Italian and international DJs, making it a must-visit for electronic music lovers.

Tip: Goa Club is relatively small, so it can get crowded. Arrive early or book a table for a more comfortable experience. The club is more about the music, so casual attire is acceptable.

Location: Via Giuseppe Libetta, 13, 00154 Roma RM, Italy
Website: www.goaclub.com

TOY ROOM CLUB

Toy Room Club is a trendy and exclusive nightclub in the heart of Rome, known for its hip-hop and R&B music nights. The club's stylish interior, coupled with its plush seating and vibrant lighting, creates an electrifying atmosphere perfect for dancing the night away. It's frequented by a chic crowd and often hosts renowned DJs, making it a top spot for nightlife enthusiasts.

Tip: Dress to impress as the club has a strict dress code. Reservations are recommended for table service, ensuring more exclusive experience.

Location: Via degli Avignonesi, 73, 00187 Roma RM,

Website: www.facebook.com/toyroomroma

QUBE DISCO

Qube Disco, set in a multi-level venue, is one of Rome's most dynamic nightclubs. Known for its themed nights and diverse music across three floors, it caters to a wide range of musical tastes. From electronic dance music to pop and indie, there's something for everyone. The club's energetic ambiance and state-of-the-art sound system make it a popular choice for locals and tourists alike.

Tip: Check out their themed nights for a unique party experience. Arriving early helps avoid long queues and ensures entry, as the club can get quite crowded later in the night.

Location: Via di Portonaccio, 212, 00159 Roma RM, Italy

Website: www.facebook.com/quberome

DA ENZO AL 29

Da Enzo al 29 is a traditional Roman trattoria located in Trastevere, offering authentic Roman cuisine. Known for its cozy atmosphere and delicious dishes like Cacio e Pepe, Carbonara, and Roman-style artichokes, it's a great spot for a late-night meal that captures the essence of Roman culinary traditions.

Tip: The restaurant is quite popular, so either book in advance or be prepared for a wait. The outdoor seating is perfect for a romantic dinner.

Location: Via dei Vascellari, 29, 00153 Roma RM, Italy
Website: www.daenzoal29.com

I SUPPLI

I Suppli is a must-visit for those craving a quick and tasty late-night snack. This establishment is famous for its 'supplì' – fried rice balls filled with tomato sauce and mozzarella. These mouth-watering treats are perfect after a night out, offering a true taste of Roman street food.

Tip: Supplì is best enjoyed hot and fresh. Don't miss out on trying their variety of flavors – each one is a delightful experience.

Location: Via di S. Francesco a Ripa, 137, 00153 Roma RM, Italy
Website: www.suppliroma.it/?lang=en

TRAPIZZINO

Trapizzino combines the concept of pizza and a sandwich, creating a unique and delicious late-night food option. Filled with various traditional Roman recipes like chicken cacciatora or eggplant parmigiana, these pocket-sized delights are a favorite among locals and tourists alike.

Tip: Trapizzino is ideal for a casual, on-the-go meal. Pair your trapizzino with a glass of local wine or a craft beer for a full experience.

Location: Multiple locations including Testaccio and Trastevere

Website: www.trapizzino.it/en/

PIZZERIA AI MARMI

Known colloquially as 'l'obitorio' (the morgue) due to its long marble tables, Pizzeria Ai Marmi is an iconic spot in Trastevere for traditional Roman pizza. This bustling pizzeria is known for its thin-crust pizzas, fried starters, and lively atmosphere, making it a popular late-night dining choice among locals and visitors.

Tip: The place is often crowded, so be prepared for a short wait. Don't miss their classic Margherita or the fried supplì as an appetizer.

Location:Viale di Trastevere, 53-59, 00153 Roma RM. Italy

Website: www.facebook.com/aimarmi/

TRASTEVERE

Trastevere is not only a charming historic district by day but also one of Rome's liveliest nightlife areas. The neighborhood's narrow streets are lined with bars, pubs, and restaurants that come alive after dark, offering a vibrant and authentic Roman nightlife experience.

Tip: Piazza di Santa Maria in Trastevere and the surrounding streets are great starting points for a night out, offering a variety of options for drinks and music.

Location: Trastevere, Rome, Italy

TESTACCIO

Testaccio is known as the heart of Rome's clubbing scene. This former working-class district has transformed into a nightlife hotspot, with a concentration of nightclubs and bars that cater to a diverse crowd. The area is particularly famous for its dance clubs and lively late-night atmosphere.

Tip: Testaccio is also known for its traditional Roman cuisine. Consider starting your evening with a hearty Roman meal before hitting the clubs.

Location: Testaccio, Rome, Italy

MONTI

Monti, a trendy and bohemian district near the Colosseum, is a favorite among the young and artistic crowd. The area is dotted with a variety of wine bars, artisanal shops, and hipster cafes. Its relaxed and creative atmosphere makes it a great place for an evening of bar-hopping and socializing with locals.

Tip: Piazza della Madonna dei Monti is a popular gathering spot in the neighborhood. Grab a drink at one of the nearby bars and join the locals lounging around the fountain.

Location: Monti, Rome, Italy

PIGNETO

Pigneto, known for its bohemian and alternative vibe, is often compared to Brooklyn in New York. This vibrant neighborhood is full of street art, eclectic bars, and trendy restaurants. Its pedestrian-only main street, Via del Pigneto, becomes a lively nights pot after dark, attracting a diverse and artsy clientele.

Tip: Explore the side streets of Pigneto to discover hidden gems in terms of bars and eateries. The area is also known for hosting live music and cultural events.

Location: Pigneto, Rome, Italy

SAFETY TIPS

Exploring Rome by night can be an exhilarating experience, but it's important to prioritize your safety to ensure your evening adventures remain pleasant memories. Here are some safety tips to keep in mind:

- **Vigilance is key**: Crowded venues and bustling streets are prime spots for pickpockets. Always be mindful of your personal belongings and consider using anti-theft bags or pouches.
- **Stay in the light**: Stick to well-lit and populated streets, especially if you're venturing out alone. Dark and deserted alleys can be risky, so it's best to avoid them.
- **Trustworthy transport**: Use only reputable taxi companies or verified ride-sharing apps for nighttime travel. It's wise to pre-save the contact details of a reliable taxi service on your phone.
- **Guard your glass**: While enjoying the local nightlife, never leave your drink unattended. Accept beverages only from trusted companions or directly from the bartender.
- **Drink smart**: Consume alcohol in moderation and stay hydrated with water throughout the night. This will help you maintain awareness and make better decisions.
- **Emergency preparedness**: Keep a list of emergency contacts, including local authorities and your embassy, easily accessible. A portable phone charger can be a lifesaver in keeping your device powered up.
- **Document safety**: Carry photocopies of your essential documents, such as your passport, and store the originals in a secure location like a hotel safe.

Remember, the night is yours to enjoy, but staying alert and prepared is the best way to ensure that your nocturnal explorations are safe and enjoyable.

By following these tips and exploring the city by night, you'll be able to experience the magic and charm of the city while staying safe and having an unforgettable time.

Rome: A Journey Through Time in Art, History, and Architecture

Rome, the capital of Italy, is a city where history, art, and architecture intermingle to create a tapestry of unparalleled cultural richness. Known as the "Eternal City," Rome's origins trace back to ancient times, evolving from a small Latin village to the heart of the powerful Roman Empire.

At the center of Rome's artistic legacy is its profound influence on the world of art, particularly during the Renaissance and Baroque periods. The city is a living gallery, adorned with works by masters like Michelangelo, Raphael, and Caravaggio. The Vatican Museums and the Sistine Chapel, with Michelangelo's iconic frescoes, are emblematic of Rome's artistic prominence. The city's streets and piazzas are dotted with sculptures and fountains by Bernini and other great artists, making art an integral part of Rome's identity.

Historically, Rome's significance is monumental. It was the center of the Roman Republic and the Roman Empire, shaping the course of Western civilization. Landmarks like the Colosseum, the Roman Forum, and the Pantheon are enduring symbols of Rome's ancient glory. The city's rich history is also marked by its role as the center of the Catholic Church, influencing religious, political, and cultural developments worldwide.

Architecturally, Rome offers a journey through various styles and epochs. From the classical grandeur of ancient Roman structures to the ornate churches and palaces of the Renaissance and Baroque, the city's architecture is a testament to its historical and artistic evolution. The St. Peter's Basilica and the Trevi Fountain are just a few examples of Rome's architectural marvels.

Rome is not just a city; it's an experience that transcends time. Each monument, artwork, and cobblestone street tells a story of a city that has been a crucible of human history. For those seeking to immerse themselves in the essence of art, history, and architecture, Rome offers an unparalleled odyssey through the annals of time.

ART AND CULTURE IN ROME

DORIA PAMPHILJ GALLERY

The Doria Pamphilj Gallery, a hidden gem in Rome's historic center, is an art lover's paradise. Housed in a splendid 17th-century palace, this privately-owned gallery presents an extraordinary collection of art, primarily from the Renaissance and Baroque periods. The gallery showcases masterpieces by renowned artists such as Caravaggio, Raphael, and Velázquez, each adding to the grandeur of the lavishly adorned rooms. The collection also includes sculptures, furniture, and decorative arts, offering a comprehensive glimpse into the artistic and cultural heritage of the era. The gallery's atmosphere, enriched by the history of the Doria Pamphilj family, provides a unique and intimate experience of viewing art.

Tip: A highlight of the visit is the Velázquez portrait of Pope Innocent X, considered one of the gallery's most significant pieces. Utilize the audio guide, which provides fascinating insights into the collection and the intriguing history of the Doria Pamphilj family. The gallery's relatively quieter environment compared to more prominent museums makes it a serene and contemplative place to appreciate art.

Location: Via del Corso, 305, 00186 Roma RM, Italy

Website: www.doriapamphilj.it/en/rome/

The MAXXI Museum, officially known as the National Museum of 21st Century Arts, stands as a beacon of contemporary art and architecture in Rome. Designed by the late Zaha Hadid, a pioneering architect, the museum itself is a masterpiece of modern design, with its innovative and dynamic structure. Inside, MAXXI dedicates itself to the promotion of contemporary creativity, showcasing a diverse array of artworks and architectural designs. The museum's permanent collection is complemented by a vibrant program of temporary exhibitions, each offering a new perspective on the current art and architectural scene. Visitors can immerse themselves in an environment where art, architecture, and culture converge to inspire dialogue and reflection.

Tip: To enhance your visit, check the museum's schedule for interactive installations, workshops, and cultural events. These activities provide an opportunity to engage with contemporary art in a dynamic and participatory way. The museum's architecture itself is a compelling reason to visit, offering a striking contrast to Rome's ancient historical backdrop. The MAXXI Museum is not just a place to view art; it's an experience that reflects the pulse of modern creativity and innovation.

Location: Via Guido Reni, 4a, 00196 Roma RM, Italy
Website: www.maxxi.art/en/

MUSEUM OF CONTEMPORARY ART OF ROME

The Museum of Contemporary Art of Rome, known as MACRO, offers a dynamic space for modern art in Rome. Located in a former brewery, the museum exhibits a variety of contemporary artworks, including installations, paintings, and multimedia projects. MACRO actively engages with the current art scene, hosting temporary exhibitions and interactive projects.

Tip: Check out the museum's rooftop terrace for a panoramic view of the city. The museum's café is a great spot to relax and reflect on the art.

Location: Via Nizza, 138, 00198 Roma RM, Italy

Website: www.museomacro.it

NATIONAL ROMAN MUSEUM

The National Roman Museum, spread across several sites in Rome, offers a comprehensive overview of the city's rich archaeological heritage. The museum's collections include an array of ancient Roman art, artifacts, mosaics, and sculptures, shedding light on Rome's historical and cultural past.

Tip: Consider which aspects of Roman history interest you the most and choose the site(s) accordingly. Palazzo Massimo is renowned for its classical sculpture collection, while Palazzo Altemps is notable for its collection of Greek and Roman sculptures.

Locations: Includes Palazzo Massimo, Palazzo Altemps, Crypta Balbi, and Baths of Diocletian

Website: www.coopculture.it/en/poi/museo-nazionale-romano

CAPITOLINE MUSEUMS

The Capitoline Museums, located on Capitoline Hill, are considered to be the world's oldest public museums. Their collections include a vast array of ancient Roman statues, inscriptions, and other artifacts, as well as paintings and sculptures from the Renaissance and Baroque periods. Highlights include the statue of Marcus Aurelius, the Capitoline Wolf, and the ruins of the ancient Temple of Jupiter.

Tip: The museums are connected by an underground gallery that leads to the Tabularium, offering a fantastic view of the Roman Forum. Plan enough time to explore both museums and the connecting gallery.

Location: Piazza del Campidoglio, 1, 00186 Roma RM

Website: www.museicapitolini.org/en

THE ARA PACIS MUSEUM

The Ara Pacis Museum is dedicated to the Altar of Peace, a monumental altar built to celebrate the peace established by Emperor Augustus. The museum, designed by architect Richard Meier, is a stunning example of contemporary architecture housing a significant relic of ancient Rome. The contrast between the modern building and the ancient altar creates a unique and fascinating dialogue.

Tip: The museum often hosts temporary art and cultural exhibitions, so check their current program. The surrounding area along the Tiber is also perfect for a scenic walk.

Location: Lungotevere in Augusta, 00186 Roma RM, Italy

Website: www.arapacis.it/en

HISTORICAL AND ARCHITECTURAL LANDMARKS IN ROME
BATHS OF CARACALLA

The Baths of Caracalla, a monumental relic of ancient Rome, offer a glimpse into the grandeur and social life of the Roman Empire. Built during the reign of Emperor Caracalla in the 3rd century AD, this vast complex was more than a mere bathing facility; it was a multifunctional center equipped with libraries, gardens, and shops, showcasing the sophistication of Roman engineering and architecture. The ruins of the baths, with their massive walls, arches, and floor mosaics, reflect the opulence that once defined this place. Walking among these remnants, visitors can imagine the baths in their full glory – a bustling gathering place for leisure and socializing. The site's size and relatively well-preserved state make it an impressive and insightful visit for those interested in ancient history and Roman culture.

Tip: A visit during the summer months is particularly special, as the Baths of Caracalla often host open-air operas and ballet performances. Experiencing a performance in this historical setting, under the stars, is an enchanting experience, blending cultural entertainment with the backdrop of ancient ruins. Additionally, exploring the baths early in the morning or later in the afternoon can offer a more tranquil experience, allowing for a leisurely exploration of the vast complex. The site's proximity to other ancient landmarks, like the Circus Maximus, makes it a worthwhile addition to an itinerary exploring Rome's ancient past.

Location: Viale delle Terme di Caracalla, 00153 Roma RM, Italy

Website: www.coopculture.it/en/poi/baths-of-caracalla/

The Appian Way, known as Via Appia Antica, is a testament to Rome's ancient engineering prowess and historical depth. Built in 312 BC, this road was one of the Roman Empire's earliest and most vital thoroughfares, stretching from Rome to Brindisi. Today, it offers a unique journey through time, flanked by ruins, catacombs, and aristocratic tombs. Visitors can walk along the same cobblestones that Roman legions once marched upon. The road is also home to significant landmarks, including the Baths of Caracalla, the Catacombs of San Callisto, and the Mausoleum of Cecilia Metella. A stroll or bike ride down the Appian Way is not just a recreational activity; it's an immersive historical experience, offering insights into the daily life and burial practices of ancient Romans. The surrounding natural landscape adds to the serene and picturesque setting, making it a peaceful escape from the bustling city center.

Tip: Exploring the Appian Way by bike allows visitors to cover more ground and access less-frequented historical sites. Bike rentals are available at various points along the route. Plan to spend at least half a day to fully appreciate the road's archaeological and natural beauty. Remember to carry water, especially during warmer months, as the area can be quite sunny with limited shade.

Location: Via Appia Antica, Rome, Italy
Website: www.parcoarcheologicoappiaantica.it

DOMUS AUREA

The Domus Aurea, or "Golden House," was Emperor Nero's vast palace complex. Today, it's an extraordinary archaeological site. The remains of this once-lavish palace offer a glimpse into the grandeur of Roman architecture and art. The recent addition of virtual reality experiences allows visitors to see the palace as it might have appeared in Nero's time.

Tip: The site is open on weekends, and visits are only possible as part of a guided tour. The VR experience is highly recommended for

a unique historical journey.

Location: Viale Serapide, 00184 Roma RM, Italy

Website: www.coopculture.it/en/poi/domus-aurea/

SANTA MARIA IN ARACOELI

The Basilica di Santa Maria in Aracoeli, a jewel atop the Capitoline Hill, is steeped in history and art. Dating back to the 6th century, this church is adorned with exquisite Byzantine mosaics and frescoes. The interior houses the revered wooden statue of the Santo Bambino, a significant religious artifact.

Visitors are greeted by a grand marble staircase leading to the church, where they can enjoy panoramic views of the Roman Forum. The serene ambiance inside the basilica, combined with its rich historical and artistic offerings, provides a reflective and awe-inspiring experience.

Tip: The church's relatively quieter atmosphere makes it an ideal place

for contemplation and appreciation of Rome's religious and cultural history.

Location: Scala dell'Arce Capitolina, 12, 00186 Roma RM, Italy

Website: www.turismoroma.it/en/places/basilica-santa-maria-aracoeli

ARCH OF CONSTANTINE

The Arch of Constantine is a triumphal arch situated between the Colosseum and the Palatine Hill. Erected by the Roman Senate to commemorate Emperor Constantine I's victory over Maxentius, this arch is one of the best-preserved Roman structures. Its rich sculptural decoration and historical reliefs provide a vivid glimpse into the art and propaganda of early 4th-century Rome.

Tip: Take a moment to appreciate the intricate carvings and reliefs that depict scenes of battle and victory, which are key to understanding the political and cultural landscape of Constantine's era.

Location: Via di S. Gregorio, 00184 Roma RM, Italy

Website: www.turismoroma.it/en/places/arch-costantine

BASILICA DI SAN GIOVANNI IN LATERANO

The Basilica di San Giovanni in Laterano (St. John Lateran Basilica) is Rome's cathedral and the official ecclesiastical seat of the Bishop of Rome, the Pope. It is considered the mother church of the Roman Catholic faithful. The basilica's architecture and interior, including its grand nave, magnificent frescoes, and the 14th-century cloister, are breathtaking.

Tip: Be sure to visit the Scala Sancta (Holy Stairs), believed to be the steps that led up to the praetorium of Pontius Pilate in Jerusalem, which Jesus Christ stood on during his Passion.

Location: P.za di S. Giovanni in Laterano, 4, 00184 Roma RM

Website: www.vatican.va/various/basiliche/san_giovanni/index_it.htm

DAY TRIPS FROM ROME

OSTIA ANTICA

Just 25 kilometers southwest of Rome, Ostia Antica offers a glimpse into ancient Roman life. This well-preserved archaeological site, once Rome's bustling port city, features ruins of homes, baths, and temples. Less crowded than Pompeii, it provides an equally fascinating

exploration of history. The ancient theater, still in use, is a highlight.

Tip: Wear comfortable shoes for exploring. Don't miss the chance to see the theater and detailed mosaics.

Location: Viale dei Romagnoli, 717, 00119 Roma RM, Italy

Website: www.ostiaantica.beniculturali.it

TIVOLI AND VILLA D'ESTE

Tivoli, located about 30 kilometers east of Rome, is famous for Villa d'Este, a UNESCO World Heritage site. This 16th-century villa is renowned for its Renaissance architecture and spectacular gardens. Its impressive fountains, waterfalls, and manicured gardens make it a delightful escape from the city.

Tip: Don't miss the famous Fountain of Neptune and the Hundred Fountains. The villa can be quite crowded on weekends, so consider a weekday visit.

Location: P.za Trento, 5, 00019 Tivoli RM, Italy

Website: www.visittivoli.eu/index.php?lang=EN

BRACCIANO AND CASTELLO ORSINI-ODESCALCHI

Bracciano is a charming small town located about 50 kilometers northwest of Rome, known for the medieval Castello Orsini-Odescalchi. The castle, overlooking Lake Bracciano, is one of the best-preserved castles in Italy and offers panoramic views. The town and the nearby lake provide a peaceful atmosphere for relaxation and exploration.

Tip: The castle is often a venue for exhibitions and cultural events. Check their schedule for any special happenings during your visit.

Location: Via Giulio Volpi, 12, 00062 Bracciano RM, Italy

Website: www.odescalchi.it

CALCATA

Calcata, about 50 kilometers north of Rome, is a unique and picturesque medieval village perched atop a volcanic cliff. The town has a bohemian vibe, with artists and creatives populating its narrow, winding streets. It's known for its artistic community, artisan shops, and quaint cafes.

Tip: The town is quite small and can be explored in a few hours, making it ideal for a leisurely afternoon trip. Enjoy the scenic views of the surrounding valley from the village.

Location: Calcata, Province of Viterbo, Lazio, Italy

Website: www.italia.it/en/lazio/viterbo/calcata

CERVETERI AND THE ETRUSCAN NECROPOLISES

Cerveteri, located about 40 kilometers northwest of Rome, is renowned for the Banditaccia Necropolis, a UNESCO World Heritage site. This ancient Etruscan burial site features thousands of tombs, including impressive tumuli (mound tombs) and underground chambers.

The necropolis offers a unique glimpse into the Etruscan civilization. **Tip**: The site is extensive, so wearing comfortable walking shoes is advisable. The National Archaeological Museum of Cerveteri nearby

is also worth a visit for further insights into the Etruscan culture.

Location: Via della Necropoli, 00052 Cerveteri RM, Italy
Website: www.italia.it/en/lazio/cerveteri/cultural-places/etruscan-necropolises-of-cerveteri

SPERLONGA

Sperlonga, about 110 kilometers southeast of Rome, is a picturesque coastal town known for its beautiful beaches and the ruins of Emperor Tiberius' villa. The town, with its whitewashed buildings and narrow alleys, offers a perfect combination of historical exploration and seaside relaxation.

Tip: The Tiberius Cave and Museum host relics and sculptures from the Roman villa. After exploring the historical sites, enjoy some time on the gorgeous beaches of Sperlonga.

Location: Sperlonga, Province of Latina, Lazio, Italy
Website: www.italia.it/en/lazio/sperlonga

FRASCATI AND THE ROMAN CASTLES

Frascati, located about 20 kilometers southeast of Rome in the Alban Hills, is famous for its villas, verdant scenery, and wine production. Part of the Castelli Romani (Roman Castles) area, it offers a pleasant escape with its cooler climate, panoramic views, and culinary delights, particularly the local Frascati wine.

Tip: Consider visiting a local vineyard for a wine tasting experience. Frascati is also known for its porchetta (roasted pork), a local culinary specialty.

Location: Frascati, Metropolitan City of Rome, Lazio, Italy

Website: www.italia.it/it/lazio/roma/frascati-castelli-romani

VITERBO

Viterbo, about 100 kilometers northwest of Rome, is a medieval city known for its well-preserved historical center, thermal springs, and Papal Palace. The city's ancient walls, medieval architecture, and charming streets make it a fascinating destination for history enthusiasts and those seeking a quieter alternative to the bustling Roman streets.

Tip: Don't miss the chance to relax in the thermal baths of the Terme dei Papi, a spa with historical roots. The San Pellegrino district, with its medieval houses and alleys, is perfect for leisurely exploration.

Location: Viterbo, Province of Viterbo, Lazio, Italy

Website: www.italia.it/en/lazio/viterbo

HADRIAN'S VILLA (VILLA ADRIANA)

Hadrian's Villa, located near Tivoli and about 30 kilometers from Rome, is an exceptional archaeological complex and a UNESCO World Heritage site. The villa, built by Emperor Hadrian in the 2nd century AD, features an array of classical buildings, pools, and gardens, reflecting the architectural tastes and innovations of its time.

Tip: Allocate several hours to explore the extensive grounds. Consider combining your visit with a trip to the nearby Villa d'Este for a full day of historical and architectural immersion.

Location: Largo Marguerite Yourcenar, 1, 00019 Tivoli RM, Italy

Website: www.visittivoli.eu/le-ville/villa-adriana&lang=EN

NAPLES AND POMPEII

A day trip to Naples and the ancient ruins of Pompeii offers a journey through rich culinary traditions and remarkable history. Naples, about 225 kilometers south of Rome, is famous for its vibrant street life, historic center, and as the birthplace of pizza. Pompeii, a short trip from Naples,

is an ancient Roman city preserved by the eruption of Mount Vesuvius, providing an unparalleled window into ancient Roman life.

Tip: The high-speed train from Rome to Naples takes about 1-1.5 hours, making this a feasible day trip. In Naples, don't miss trying authentic Neapolitan pizza. Pompeii is vast, so wearing comfortable shoes is recommended.

Location: Naples and Pompeii, Campania, Italy

Website: www.italia.it/en/campania/naples

END NOTE

As we conclude this guide to Rome, it becomes clear that the Eternal City is more than a mere travel destination; it's a vibrant mosaic of history, culture, and timeless beauty. Rome, with its streets echoing millennia of history, invites you to delve into an array of experiences, from the awe-inspiring Colosseum to the serene paths of Villa Borghese. This city is a living museum, where each ancient stone tells a story, and every cobblestoned alley whispers legends of empires and artistry.

Rome's narrative is a complex tapestry of its glorious past and its lively present. The majestic ruins of the Roman Forum coexist with the lively buzz of Trastevere, creating a unique juxtaposition of the ancient and the contemporary. The city's architecture, a striking amalgamation of historical monuments and modern vitality, mirrors Rome's respect for its heritage and its ongoing evolution.

The culinary journey in Rome is as rich and varied as its landscapes. From quaint trattorias serving classic Roman fare to innovative restaurants redefining gastronomy, the city is a haven for food lovers. Its cuisine is a celebration of flavors, deeply rooted in tradition and the local bounty.

Leaving Rome, you carry more than memories; you take with you a piece of its spirit. The echoes of ancient gladiators, the serenity of the Tiber, the taste of authentic gelato, and the splendor of Renaissance art linger long after your departure. You leave behind the majestic Vatican, the romantic Spanish Steps, and the warmth of its people, but with the knowledge that Rome is a city to revisit, time and again.

Rome stands as a testament to the resilience and passion of its people. It's a city that embraces life in all its facets, a place where the grandeur of history and the joy of the present coexist in harmony. Rome is a destination for all, a city that reveals its wonders and familiar delights with each visit.

As this guide concludes, remember that Rome isn't just the end of a journey; it's an ongoing exploration. It's a city that remains with you, calling you back to rediscover and re-experience its enchantment. Rome awaits your next visit with open arms and a promise: the magic of this city is everlasting, and each return will be as mesmerizing as the first.

Embark on your journey through this historical gem, and let the enduring allure of Rome inspire you, today and always.

EXTRA RESOURCES

Rome
maps

Rome
General Map

Rome
Tourist Map

Rome City
Center
Map

Rome
Sightseeing
Map

Rome and
surroundings
Transport Map

Rome
Railway Map

ATAC
(Public
Transport
in Rome)

Roma Tourist
Pass

Official Tourism
Website of Rome

Official Vatican
Website

TRAVEL

PLACES TO SEE:

LOCAL FOOD TO TRY:

DAY 1

DAY 2

DAY 3

DAY 4

DAY 5

DAY 6

NOTES

PLANNER

Loved Your Journey With Our Guide? ⭐
Your feedback makes a world of difference! If our guide helped you explore or enjoy your destination, we would be thrilled if you could take a moment to leave us a 5-star review on our product page.🙏

Simply click the link or go to any of our product pages on your preferred retailer website and **share your recommendations.**
https://www.amazon.com/stores/Tailored-Travel-Guides/author/B0C4TV5TZX

Scan the QR Code to share your recommendations

Join our Tailored Travel Guides Network
for more benefits by accessing this link:
https://mailchi.mp/d151cba349e8/ttgnetwork
Or by scanning the QR code

Thank you for chosing Tailored Travel Guides!

Discover Your Journey

UNLOCK A WORLD OF UNFORGETTABLE EXPERIENCES WITH TAILORED TRAVEL GUIDES!

As your go-to source for personalized and meticulously crafted travel guides, we ensure that every adventure is uniquely yours. Our team of dedicated travel experts and local insiders design each guide with your preferences, interests, and travel style in mind, providing you with the ultimate customized travel experience.

Embark on your next journey with confidence, knowing that Tailored Travel Guides has got you covered. To explore more exceptional destinations and discover a treasure trove of additional guides, visit www.tailoredtravelguides.com. or our collection available on:

Amazon at this link: www.amazon.com/stores/Tailored-Travel-Guides/author/B0C4TV5TZX or on **Google Play**, at this link: https://play.google.com/store/books/author?id=Tailored+Travel+Guides on **Etsy**, at this link: https://tailoredtravelguides.etsy.com

Happy travels, and here's to a lifetime of remarkable memories!

ALSO IN THE SERIES

Turin

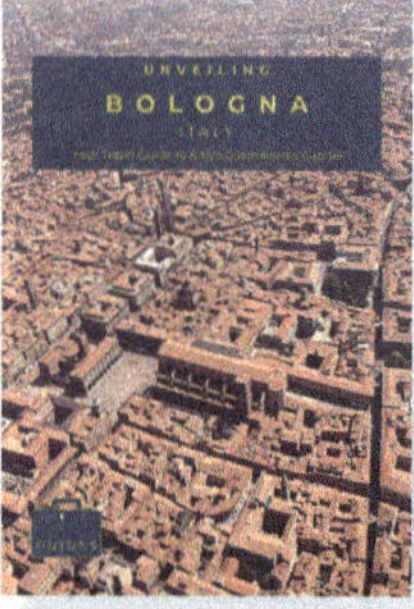

Bologna

Rome

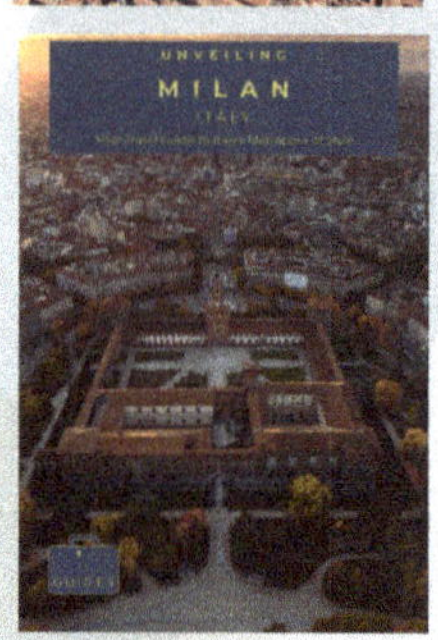

Milan

Genoa

Venice

Verona

Florence

Naples

Palermo

CHECK OUT THE SPAIN UNVEILED SERIES

Malaga

Barcelona

Valencia

Seville

Cordoba

Bilbao

Toledo

San Sebastian

Madrid

Tenerife

Granada

CHECK OUT THE FRANCE UNVEILED SERIES

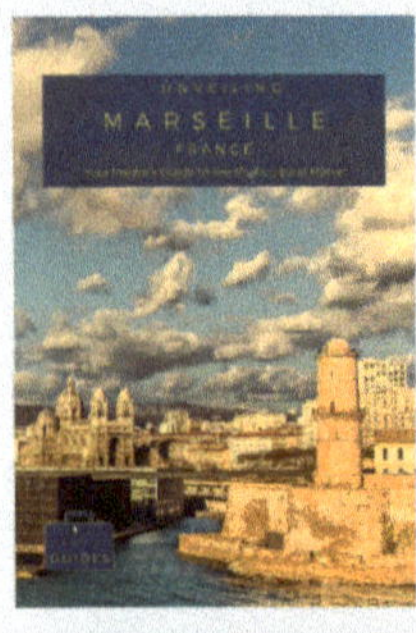

Marseille

Nantes

Toulouse

Nice

Paris

Lille

Lyon

Montpellier

Bordeaux

Strasbourg